Drift and Mastery

Drift and Mastery

An Attempt to Diagnose the Current Unrest

Walter Lippmann

"Men find themselves working and thinking and feel-
ing in relation to an environment, which . . . is
without precedent in the history of the world."
Graham Wallas, The Great Society

With a revised introduction and notes
by WILLIAM E. LEUCHTENBURG

The University of Wisconsin Press

Published 1985

The University of Wisconsin Press
114 North Murray Street
Madison, Wisconsin 53715

The University of Wisconsin Press, Ltd.
1 Gower Street
London WC1E 6HA, England

First Wisconsin printing
This edition first published in 1981 by Prentice-Hall, Inc.,
Englewood Cliffs, New Jersey 07632
Originally published in 1914 by Mitchell Kennerley

Printed in the United States of America

ISBN 0-299-10604-7 paper; LC 85-40764

A Note About This Edition

The original edition of *Drift and Mastery* was published by Mitchell Kennerley in 1914. Save for the deletion or rearrangement of a few footnotes, this new edition follows faithfully the original text. I am grateful to Howard Gottlieb, Librarian of the Historical Manuscripts Collection, Sterling Memorial Library, Yale University, for permitting me to consult the original handwritten draft of *Drift and Mastery* in the Library's Lippmanniana collection.

W.E.L.

Table of Contents

Drift and Mastery

Walter Lippmann's *Drift and Mastery*

Seldom does a work by an author only just turned twenty-five attract the kind of attention accorded Walter Lippmann's *Drift and Mastery* when it first appeared in the fall of 1914. Randolph Bourne, who sometimes dipped his pen in acid, called it "a book one would have given one's soul to have written," while the distinguished Supreme Court Justice, Oliver Wendell Holmes, never one to settle for less than the very best, confided, "I read nothing to speak of here, but one of the young men I delight in has just sent me *Drift and Mastery* . . . that I think devilish well written, full of articulation of the impalpable and unutterable, . . . altogether a delightful fresh piece of writing and thinking." Still more unrestrained were the encomiums of Theodore Roosevelt, who put *Drift and Mastery* in a category with Bryce's classic, *The American Commonwealth*. "No man who wishes seriously to study our present social, industrial and political life can afford not to read it through and through and ponder and digest it," he declared. Lippmann, the former President explained to a foreign diplomat, was "a personal friend of mine . . . [who] is, I think, on the whole the most brilliant man of his age in all the United States."

Heady words for certain, but Lippmann had been hearing them for some years because he was, by all accounts, one of the most gifted undergraduates to attend Harvard in this century. He raced through college in three years picking up a Phi Beta Kappa key on the way. He stayed on in Cambridge a fourth year, though, as an assistant to George Santayana, and also got to know William James when one of Lippmann's pieces in a campus journal inspired the philosopher to cross the Yard for an unannounced call on the student in his lodgings. The visiting British lecturer Graham Wallas, a Fabian Socialist of international renown, was so taken with Lippmann that he adopted him as his protégé and was later to start his influential *The Great Society* with the exceptional rubric of an open letter to the young American.

1

Both James and Santayana influenced Lippmann deeply. Although he never took courses with James, he joined students in talks at the philosopher's home. He found particularly appealing James's open-mindedness and his willingness to give all creeds a hearing. Excited by James's conception of a universe still in the process of creation, he was moved most of all by the philosopher's call to make choices and act now instead of waiting until the never-to-be day when one had all the evidence. Yet he did not become a thoroughgoing Jamesian. In later years, Lippmann said that it was Santayana, who regarded him, along with T. S. Eliot, as one of his brightest students, who saved him from becoming a unequivocal pragmatist. Throughout his life, Lippmann sought an order in the universe which the intellectual with aesthetic sensibility could articulate for a society uncertain of its goals.

Neither James nor Santayana, though, affected Lippmann nearly so much as Graham Wallas did. A leader of the Fabians for twenty years and a political activist, Wallas had come to believe that the approach of the English Socialists had failed because it was based on an unrealistic view of human nature. He sought to achieve a departure in political thought by grounding politics on the recognition that people often acted on irrational impulses. His lecture at Harvard on the relation of psychology and politics in the spring of 1910 opened up to Lippmann a new way of thinking about political conflict. Although James had made much the same point, it was from Wallas that Lippmann learned the importance of putting man—man as he really was: often perverse, mercurial, illogical—at the center of any theory of politics.

To a degree Wallas could make the impact he did because he and Lippmann were both socialists, skeptical socialists to be sure but socialists all the same. As a sophomore, Lippmann had responded to a call for volunteers to help tenement families whose homes had been razed by a fire. Shocked by the poverty of the Chelsea slums, he had read avidly the writings of G. B. Shaw and H. G. Wells. Soon he was helping organize a Socialist Club at Harvard and serving as its president. Other members included Heywood Broun, the poet Alan Seeger, and Robert Edmond Jones, soon to be launched on an illustrious career as a stage designer. John Reed, then more bohemian than radical, attended meetings but did not join. The club, not content to be the usual Marxist discussion group, acted with remarkable vigor for an undergraduate group in this era; it condemned the university for paying low wages to its help, petitioned for a new course in socialism, and even sponsored bills in the Massachusetts legislature. Young Lippmann also cut quite a figure in the meetings of the Intercollegiate Socialist Society; when he spoke at Columbia, Randolph Bourne turned up to hear him.

In 1910 Lippmann came into the orbit of yet another magnetic figure. Late that summer, Lincoln Steffens went up to Cambridge to hire a cub reporter to do legwork for the muckraking pieces he was writing for *Every-body's*. He announced that he was looking for "the ablest mind that could express itself in writing." Everyone told him Lippmann was the man he wanted; after talking to him, Steffens agreed. The precocious Lippmann quickly proved himself to Steffens's skeptical colleagues, and he soon made a place for himself on the magazine. He could write exceptionally well, and Steffens showed him how to write still better. Steffens also altered Lippmann's view of reform politics. Lippmann met the veteran muckraker at a time when he had become disillusioned with endless journalistic exposés. Steffens taught Lippmann the inadequacy of relying on exposures and schooled him in the need to develop analyses that were more penetrating and more constructive.

In New York, Lippmann joined the Socialist Party, an event that led to the only excursion into politics he was ever to take. Early in 1912, the New York Socialist leader Morris Hillquit persuaded George Lunn, the recently elected Socialist mayor of Schenectady, to appoint Lippmann his assistant. That assignment gave the young journalist his first real opportunity to try out his theories, to abandon the study and the editorial room, and to plunge into political life. Lippmann lasted only a few months. He found the people whom Lunn sought to lead into the ideal commonwealth indifferent and prejudiced; they did not behave at all the way he had been led to expect The People would act. Never again would he involve himself directly in a political movement.

Lippmann left Schenectady still a socialist, but an unenthusiastic one. He had little patience with the dull, painful struggle of the gas and water Socialists to win superficial reforms. His socialist comrades thought they were fighting "Special Privilege," he commented "But to me it always seemed that we were like Peer Gynt struggling against a formless Boyg—invisible yet everywhere." If he was disturbed by the gradualist approach of the moderate socialists, he was even more troubled by Marxist dogmatism. He emerged from his socialist encounter with a dislike of absolutist solutions and rigid utopias that would mark his writings from his first books to *The Good Society*. He came increasingly to fear that Socialism would lead to the establishment of an omnicompetent state that had "within it the germs of that great bureaucratic tyranny which Chesterton and Belloc have named the Servile State."

After his Schenectady disappointment, Lippmann went to the Maine woods to clear his thoughts. There in the summer of 1912 he shared a cabin with his friend, Alfred Booth Kuttner, who was translating Freud's *Interpretation of Dreams* into English. As Kuttner, who had been a patient of Dr. A. A. Brill, Freud's leading disciple in America, turned out his translation, Lippmann went over it with him. Together they discussed the implications of Freud's theories. Lippmann, already schooled by Wallas in the significance of the irrational, immediately joined the ranks of the Freudians, and he did much to win acceptance for Freudian ideas in this country. It was at Lippmann's suggestion that Mabel Dodge invited Dr. Brill to speak at her Greenwich Village salon. The Freudians were equally taken with Lippmann. His first book got an enthusiastic review from Ernest Jones in *Imago*, Freud's organ in Vienna.

A Preface to Politics drew upon both Lippmann's awareness of the fresh winds of doctrine that were blowing across the Atlantic and his experiences in Manhattan where, for a season, he fell in with a band of radical young intellectuals. Disillusioned with socialism, he nonetheless continued to feel the lure of political rebellion. He went to Mabel Dodge's salon, took part in labor demonstrations, and wrote for the *Masses*. He still admired writers such as Herbert Croly, whose *A Promise of American Life,* with its reliance on a strong national government and its acceptance of the inevitability of trusts, gave ideological coherence to Teddy Roosevelt's New Nationalism. But he was more attracted to those European thinkers—especially Freud but also Henri Bergson, Friedrich Nietzsche, and Georges Sorel—who confirmed his distrust of nineteenth-century rationalism. When *A Preface to Politics* was published in 1913, it revealed, sometimes transparently, his debt to these writers. A dazzling performance for a young man of twenty-three, just two years out of college, it demonstrated less Lippmann's originality than his actute sensitivity to the *dernier cri.*

The book was a "preface" in that it strove not to present a political program but to explain the novel ways of thinking that must precede the creation of a new politics. *A Preface to Politics* is the outcry of a young rebel against those venerable but antiquated institutions that thwarted spontaneity and dammed up the bursting energies of men. Men should view themselves not as the pawns of folkways, Lippmann declared, but as innovators who can use their imaginations to shape their environment.

A Preface to Politics distinguished between the "routineer," who slavishly followed precedent, and the inventor. The routineers, Lippmann maintained, had used "the sterile tyranny of the taboo" to smother impulses, when they should have recognized that "every lust is capable of some civilized impression." Instead of channeling desire in the right direction, the routineer forbade it; he had fought against the emerging trusts back in the 1880s and he now was fighting against the emerging unions. Whenever he was faced with a new expression of man's urge for change, he enacted another statute to deny it. "The routineer in a panic," Lippmann wrote, "turns to a taboo." In showing how rigid respect for the ways of yesteryear could inhibit political creativity, Lippmann came dangerously close to denying tradition any value at all. "The institutions of the past," he had written in 1912, "are like the fresh eggs of the past—good while they are fresh." Even more, Lippmann's celebration of the autonomous, untrammeled will ran the peril of embracing outright anti-intellectualism. These tendencies distressed no one more than his mentor, Graham Wallas, who took the extraordinary step of chiding him publicly for his errors. Published in June 1914, *The Great Society* was read by Lippmann in manuscript. In the open letter to Lippmann with which Wallas began the book, he noted that he had been disturbed by some of the implications of his earlier *Human Nature and Politics* and had written this latest volume as, in part, "an argument against certain forms of twentieth-century anti-intellectualism." "I am sending this new book to you," he wrote at the end of his letter to Lippmann, "in the hope that it may be of some help to you when you write that sequel to your *Preface to Politics* for which all your friends are looking."

Wallas did more than give his youthful disciple the impetus to write his second book; he found him a place to write it. At a village inn in Surrey in the summer of 1913, Lippmann sat down to begin his labors. Though he worked at a breakneck pace, he returned to America with the project unfinished, and it was not until the following June, once more at his retreat in the Maine woods, that he made the final emendations. He entitled his latest effort, *Drift and Mastery*.

Meantime, Lippmann had been given still more reason to regard himself as a comer. In the fall of 1913, Croly had paid him the honor of inviting him to lunch at an elite New York club in order to ask him to join the staff of a new magazine which was being launched under Croly's editorship; it was to be called *The New Republic*. Lippmann, Croly wrote a learned jurist some weeks later, "does not know quite as much as he might, but he knows a lot and his general sense of values is excellent. He has enough real feeling, conviction, and knowledge to give a certain assurance, almost a certain dignity to his impertinence, and, of course, the ability to get away with impertinence is almost the best quality a political journalist can have." Croly added: "I consider him a gift from Heaven. . . . I don't know where I could find a substitute with so much innocence of conviction united with so much critical versatility." The first issue of *The New Republic*, with Lippmann's name on the masthead, appeared in November 1914 at almost the same moment as the publication of *Drift and Mastery*.

In his second book Lippmann got away with no little "impertinence." He subtitled it nothing less than "An Attempt to Diagnose the Current Unrest," a fair amount of territory for a twenty-five-year-old to survey. And, though his diagnosis departed drastically from what he had published little more than a year earlier, he confessed no error. One commentator has remarked that "the fact that Lippmann could discard without the least compunction most of the notions he had embraced so heartily in *A Preface to Politics* could reasonably be interpreted as the mark of a mind more pliant than critical," and another has stated, "Perhaps what bothers me most is Lippmann's air of assurance when he is reversing his field, as he often did, or when he relies upon antitheses . . . when what is needed is the making of distinctions." Yet another writer, Ronald Steel, in his superb biography of Lippmann, has said of *Drift and Mastery:* "After earlier dismissing logic, Lippmann now decried the 'widespread attempt to show the futility of ideas'—a fair complaint, but one that could have been directed most pointedly against his own *Preface to Politics.*" Though *Drift and Mastery* did not altogether repudiate the emphases of *A Preface to Politics,* it unmistakably bore the marks of Wallas's gentle censure. In a year, Lippmann had moved from Bergson's élan vital to the scientific method. To be sure, he continued to insist that any viable political theory must face up to the irrational in man. "Criticism will have to slough off the prejudices of the older rationalism if it is to have any radical influence on ideas," he wrote. "Men's desires are not something barbaric which the intellect must shun. Their desires are what make their lives, they are what move and govern." Indeed, he said, "if thinking didn't serve desire, it would be the most useless occupation in the world." But in *Drift and Mastery,* Lippmann looked no longer to intuition or the creative myth but to science. "Mastery" meant making the scientific spirit the discipline of democracy, he asserted. In this new book, he mentioned Sorel not at all, and went out of his way to break lances with Bergson. "A mere emotion of futurity, that sense of 'vital urge' which is so common today, will fritter itself away unless it comes under the scientific discipline, where men use language accurately, know fact from fancy, search out their own prejudice, are willing to learn from failures, and do not shrink from the long process of close observation," Lippmann stated. "Rightly understood science is the culture under which people can live forward in the midst of complexity, and treat life not as something given but something to be shaped."

In years to come, the belief that science will save us would appear to Lippmann to be quite wrongheaded, but at the moment he lavished on it all the attention he had earlier given to the irrational. "Democracy in politics is the twin-brother of scientific thinking," he claimed. "They had to come together. As absolutism falls, science arises. It *is* self-government. For when the impulse which overthrows kings and priests and unquestioned creeds becomes self-conscious we call it science. . . . The scientific spirit is the discipline of democracy, the escape from drift, the outlook of a free man."

As these comments on the demise of secular and clerical hegemony suggest, *Drift and Mastery* also differed from its predecessor in another critical respect. No longer was the tyranny of the establishment the chief menace to freedom. On the contrary, the old order had been overthrown, Lippmann insisted. "The sanctity of property, the patriarchal family, hereditary caste, the dogma of sin, obedience to authority,—the rock of ages, in brief has been blasted for us," he said. "The dominant forces in our world are not the sacredness of property, nor the intellectual leadership of the priest; they are not the divinity of the constitution, the glory of industrial push, Victorian sentiment, New England respectability, the Republican Party, or John D. Rockefeller. . . . We have scotched the romance of success." No transformation impressed Lippmann so much as the altered status of private property. In a brilliant anticipation of Berle and Means, he pointed out that in the modern corporation, ownership was rapidly being separated from control. "The trust movement," Lippmann observed, "is doing what no conspirator or revolutionist could ever do: it is sucking the life out of private property." A new class of managers had arisen with institutional interests and attitudes quite different from those of the old profiteer. "The managers are on salary, divorced from ownership and from bargaining," he pointed out. "They represent the revolution in business incentives at its very heart. For they conduct gigantic enterprises and they stand outside the higgling of the market, outside the shrewdness and strategy of competition. The motive of profit is not their personal motive. That is an astounding change."

In truth, Lippmann's historical perspective invited close scrutiny. Quite apart from his implicit assumption that so much had changed in twelve months, he so telescoped the past that the struggle against the authority of the Vatican during the Reformation and the overturning of absolute monarchy in the eighteenth century appeared to be events of the past generation. In glorifying the industrial statesmanship of U. S. Steel, he ignored the reality that steel magnates continued to have an avid appetite for profits. And if Lippmann himself was far along on the road that took him from *bar mitzvah* to nonbelief, millions of Americans still regarded the rituals of religion as indispensable.

Yet by assuming that Americans were already liberated, Lippmann gave himself license to pose an arresting question: Once you have achieved freedom, what do you do with it? He assumed that this was an inquiry that both the nation and the individual needed to answer, though he sometimes left the connection between the two obscure. No longer hampered by traditional constraints, the nation now had to find a common "democratic purpose," he asserted. And each of its citizens confronted a similar task, for a man "can't . . . live with any meaning unless he formulates for himself a vision of what is to come out of the unrest."

In delineating the predicament of the individual, Lippmann composed several of his most eloquent passages in words that continue to speak to us today. "All of us are immigrants spiritually," he wrote. "The modern man is not yet settled in his world. It is strange to him, terrifying, alluring, and incomprehensibly big." Like Matthew Arnold's bereft wayfarer on Dover Beach, stripped of certitude on a darkling plain, "we are unsettled to the very roots of our being. There isn't a human relation, whether of parent and child, husband and wife, worker and employer, that doesn't move in a strange situation. . . . There are no precedents to guide us, no wisdom that wasn't made for a simpler age."

7

Neither individual nor nation could hope to regain any sense of certitude unless the tendency toward "drift" was overcome, Lippmann warned. A useful metaphor, "drift" permitted him to settle his scores with a number of attitudes he had come to deplore. The drifters included the utopians with their idle dreams of a future Paradise to be achieved without effort, the socialist visionaries who believed in the inevitability of their future triumph, the purveyors of Adam Smith economics who had lost touch with the age, and the conservative philistines smugly satisfied with routine. Most of Lippmann's arrows, though, were reserved for those who imagined that it was still possible to retain the "village culture" of what they misremembered as a golden age. It was that fantasy that made William Jennings Bryan "so irresistibly funny to sophisticated newspaper men," Lippmann said. "He is the true Don Quixote of our politics, for he moves in a world that has ceased to exist."

Unlike Secretary of State Bryan, President Woodrow Wilson knew better, Lippmann stated, but he was no less mischievous for, despite recognizing that things had changed, he wanted to return the country to the nineteenth-century world of free enterprise, a world Wilson misperceived as embodying the quintessence of liberty. "You would think that competitive commercialism was really a generous, chivalrous, high-minded stage of human culture," Lippmann said. Wilson, Lippmann protested, spoke for "the man on the make" but had never a word of understanding for the new type of administrator, for the professionally trained businessman, or for the importunate demands of labor. The president did not seem to grasp at all that it might be necessary "to organize the fundamental industries of the country on some definite plan." Hostile to the "larger, collective life upon which the world is entering," Wilson returned constantly to his single-minded ambition for the would-be entrepreneur. Though he spoke of a "New Freedom," Wilson saw the working man "merely as a possible shopkeeper," Lippmann said. "That is the push and force of this New Freedom, a freedom for the little profiteer, but no freedom for the nation from the narrowness, the poor incentives the limited vision of small competitors—no freedom from . . . the chaos, the welter, the strategy of industrial war."

The New Freedom erred so grievously, Lippmann declared, because it failed to recognize that the profit motive was a poor incentive for creating the good society. "Private commercialism is an antiquated, feeble, mean, and unimaginative way of dealing with the possibilities of modern industry," he wrote. Lippmann added: "Modern industry was created by the profiteer, and here it is, the great fact of our lives, blackening our cities, fed with the lives of children, a tyrant over men and women, turning out enormous stocks of produce, good, bad, and horrible." In sum, he observed, "Wherever civilization is seen to be in question, the Economic Man of commercial theorists is in dispute."

8

In place of these unworthy values that he associated with "drift," Lippmann enunciated the Promethean theme of "mastery," a Jamesian emphasis on a purposive attempt to manipulate one's environment, indeed to create the unfinished universe in which one lives. *Drift and Mastery* not only repeated the warning of *A Preface to Politics* that tradition and routine smother spontaneity, but cautioned that the revolutionary situation confronting the nation required the shaping of new instruments. "To do this men have to substitute purpose for tradition: and that is, I believe, the profoundest change that has ever taken place in human history," Lippmann wrote. "We can no longer treat life as something that has trickled down to us. We have to deal with it deliberately, devise its social organization, alter its tools, formulate its method, educate and control it. In endless ways we put intention where custom has reigned. We break up routine, make decisions, choose our ends, select means." The promise of the future, Lippmann argued, lay neither in the mean conceptions of the profiteer nor in the fantasies of the revolutionist, but in replacing the profit motive with the pride of craftsmanship and sense of service of the professional man. "What is the meaning of these protean efforts to supersede the profiteer," he asked "if not that his motive produces results hostile to use, and that he is a usurper where the craftsman, the inventor and the industrial statesman should govern?"

Lippmann's allusion to the "industrial statesman" indicated that he saw signs that some creative individuals were already making the necessary adjustments to the demands of the age. In *A Preface to Politics*, Lippmann had noted that business leadership had passed into "the hands of men interested in production as a creative art instead of as brute exploitation." That "subtle fact," he observed, "may civilize the whole class conflict." In *Drift and Mastery*, he developed this conception more fully. It was no accident, Lippmann commented, "that the universities have begun to create graduate schools of business-administration." Business was "becoming a profession with university standing equal to that of law, medicine, or engineering." As a consequence, he concluded, "the instincts of workmanship, of control over brute things, the desire for order, the satisfaction of services rendered and uses created, the civilizing passions are given a chance to temper the primal desire to have and to hold and to conquer."

Yet Lippmann knew better than to place all of his faith in the transformation of the businessman. "Nothing would be easier than to shout for joy, and say that everything is about to be fine: the business men are undergoing a change of heart," he wrote. He was wryly skeptical of the "mystic and rhetorical commercialism" of the public relations men, and he perceived, too, that in many corporations, control had passed not to a professionally minded class of managers but to financiers. Moreover, if he did not fully see the dangers lurking in what James Burnham was later to call "the managerial revolution," he had enough sophistication to recognize the need to check concentrated business power with the countervailing power of labor; of the consumer (especially as mobilized by women); and, more problematically, of the State. "Without unions," Lippmann wrote, "industrial democracy is unthinkable." Only the organization of working men prevented the creation of "a permanent, servile class." The tactics of union leaders, Lippmann conceded, were often crude and violent, but what did you expect? Since they were employed where "life is nakedly brutal," their manners were not of the parlor but of the frontier. "It seems to me simply that the effort to build up unions is as much the work of pioneers, as the extension of civilization into the wilderness," he remarked. "The unions are the first feeble effort to conquer the industrial jungle for democratic life." The more power unions achieved, the more "reasonable" they would become. "Reason begins," Lippmann noted, "when men have enough power to command respect; a co-operative solution of industrial problems is possible only when all the partners to the co-operation must listen to each other."

Drift and Mastery did not mark the first time that Lippmann had championed the cause of labor, but in this instance he made a distinction that he had not insisted upon before. Perhaps nothing in America better expressed the spontaneity Lippmann had urged in *A Preface to Politics* than the rebellious mood of the IWW. Lippmann himself had participated with John Reed and others in producing a Madison Square Garden pageant to dramatize the strike of the Paterson silk workers. In *Drift and Mystery*, though, Lippmann brushed aside "Big Bill" Haywood and the tactics of the IWW. The violence of the Wobblies, he believed, was an index to their weakness. In the railway brotherhoods, on the other hand, one heard very little mutinous talk, Lippmann noted; hence, radical labor leaders dismissed them as conservative. "That is a very interesting accusation," Lippmann responded. "The railroad men have won wages and respect far beyond anything that the IWW can hope for. They have power which makes the IWW look insignificant." For mastery to be achieved, he contended, labor, like business, required "discipline."

If Lippmann saw potentialities in a mature labor movement, he placed even greater emphasis on the organized consumer. Today, the anticipation that "the consumer" would lead the nation to a promised land seems chimerical, and even in his own day, Lippmann had to acknowledge the objection of the radicals that the notion of a consumer interest was mythical and sentimental. Lippmann countered: "But we are finding, I think, that the real power emerging today in democratic politics is just the mass of the people who are crying out against the 'high cost of living.' That is a consumer's cry. Far from being an impotent one, it is, I believe, destined to be stronger than the interests either of labor or of capital." He said further: "With the consumer awake, neither the worker nor the employer can use politics for his special interest. The public, which is more numer-

ous than either side, is coming to be the determining force in government." No longer an active socialist, but unwilling to settle for the homilies
of conservatism, Lippmann, in advancing the conception of a consumer
interest, reflected the progressives' hope to evade or resolve class conflicts
by finding a public interest, even a general will, that could be imposed on
society.

Lippmann's discussion of the consumer also gave him a fulcrum for
dealing with the women's movement, a topic he addressed with some am-
biguity. He had no doubt that women were on their way to being emancipated, but he attributed that welcome development not to the struggle of
the feminists but to impersonal forces. He thought that the inequality of
women harmed both sexes, children, and the republic, but he dreaded the
prospect of women at work. "I, for one, should say that the presence of
women in the labor market is an evil to be combatted by every means at
our command," Lippmann wrote. (Confusingly, however, he spoke at another point of the value of careers for women.) "Mastery" implied instead
"the application of the arts and sciences to a deepened and more extensively organized home," through such measures as collective shopping and
day care centers. Although he believed women would improve the civic
culture by participating in politics, he anticipated that they would do so
chiefly as housewives who did the family marketing. "They have more time
for politics than men," Lippmann declared, "and it is no idle speculation
to say that their influence will make the consumer the real master of the
political situation."

Lippmann appeared to be even more ambiguous about what "mastery"
implied for the role of the State. At times he expressed sentiments appropriate to a man who had not yet severed his ties to the Socialist Party. He
wrote of the advisability of drawing up a national plan to develop natural
resources, said that there was every reason to believe that price fixing
would be extended to the great industries; mentioned offhandedly that
the day was likely to come when the government would be operating the
basic industries; and remarked that "collectivism or 'state socialism' is perhaps the chief instrument of the awakened consumer." In his praise of "the
administrator," he could be thought to be writing the bible of that new
class of political men who stepped onto the stage for the first time in the
twentieth century: the Gifford Pinchots of the Progressive era, the Rex-
ford Tugwells of the New Deal. But if that was Lippmann's point, he was
curiously diffident about making it. He wrote about the trusts being driven
into line by the American people, but he never said how they were to do
it. He suggested that voters could "dominate great industrial organizations," but he did not say how. He mentioned "the whole possibility of the
state" but did not reveal what that possibility was, save in a few unadorned
sentences. When he did praise the new class of administrators, the context
suggested that he was talking not about the Pinchots but about the man-

agers of U. S. Steel. And he scoffed at the notion that you could "institute a better industrial order by decree." Hence, different writers have been able to see in *Drift and Mastery* either a lucid statement of advanced progressivism or an apologia for a new business elite. In brief, *Drift and Mastery* is not without flaws. Its historical assumptions are suspect, its presentation of ideas sometimes opaque. It is not at all clear what Lippmann means, for example, when he writes a sentence such as, "Mastery, whether he like it or not, is an immense collaboration, in which all the promises of to-day will have their vote." There is also a great deal of critical importance that he leaves out. He has nothing at all to say about race, or, in the very year of Sarajevo, about foreign affairs, a subject on which he was to become an authority. Lippmann himself described his first two books at the time as "both prolegomena—terribly inadequate," and nearly a half-century later he dismissed *Drift and Mastery* as a "freshman effort."

Nonetheless, *Drift and Mastery* may well prove to be the most enduring of all of Lippmann's many works. In later years Lippmann would write more ponderous books, some of which still bear rereading, but by then he had become more set in his ways, more subdued by the weight of events, more disapproving of the State, less interested in working people, less sanguine about human nature, and, not infrequently, more self-satisfied. In earlier writings, notably in *A Preface to Politics*, his mood had been more insurrectionary. *Drift and Mastery* catches him in midpassage, at that moment when, though somewhat chastened, he embraces life in a buoyant spirit.

Not at all unaware of the depressing evidence of "drift," he wrote as an optimistic young critic confident that he could show the way toward that "mastery" that would assure a brighter tomorrow. "In a real sense it is an adventure," he declared. "We have still to explore the new scale of human life which machinery has thrust upon us. . . . We have still to adapt our abilities to immense tasks." He did not doubt that the future could be approached without dread for "America is pre-eminently the country where there is practical substance in Nietzsche's advice that we should live not for our fatherland but for our children's land." As David Hollinger has observed in an incisive essay, "*Drift and Mastery's* tradition was that of Emerson's belief in the ability of the human mind to make reality, not the skeptical tradition of Emerson's critic, Melville; there was no White Whale in the young Lippmann's cosmos, waiting for a chance to bring human hopes down to size."

But it was far from being a fatuous book. Indeed, Lippmann stressed over and over the bewildering perplexities confronting mortals in the modern world. "We are an uprooted people," he wrote, "newly arrived, and *nouveau riche*." Not at all content with the nostrums of the reformers, he warned that "the emancipated woman has to fight something worse than the crusted prejudices of her uncles; she has to fight the bewilderment in her own soul." In words that sound more appropriate to what decades later would be called the age of anxiety, Lippmann declared: "No mariner ever enters upon a more uncharted sea than does the average human being born into the twentieth century. Our ancestors thought they knew their way from birth through all eternity; we are puzzled about the day after to-morrow."

Indeed, much of the excitement of reading *Drift and Mastery* today derives from the fact that Lippmann was so self-consciously aware that he belonged to a new generation facing for the first time the problems of modern America, much the same questions we now confront. If Lippmann had merely written a tract about politics and the trusts, it would hold little interest save for his biting critique of the New Freedom. But he speaks directly to us because he conveys that sense of first impressions of a newfound world which is our own universe.

Yet though Lippmann viewed himself as the tribune of modernity, he gave some indications that he was not altogether comfortable with the way that urban, industrial forces had transformed the land. He catalogued the evidence of "vulgarity" in the nation: "the amusements of the city; the jokes that pass for jokes; the blare that stands for beauty, the folksongs of Broadway," and he lamented "the deceptive clamor that disfigures the scenery, covers fences, plasters the city, and blinks and winks at you through the night." He expressed his disgust at "the eastern sky ablaze with chewing gum, the northern with tooth-brushes and underwear, the western with whiskey, and the southern with petticoats, the whole heavens brilliant with monstrously flirtatious women" and at magazines "in which a rivulet of text trickles through meadows of automobiles, baking powders, corsets and kodaks."

Perhaps more than in any of his other writings we are aware in *Drift and Mastery* of tensions in Lippmann's approach, especially between reason and emotion. Lippmann was moving away from the accent on the nonrational of *A Preface to Politics,* but he had not yet wholly abandoned it. He was singing the praises of the scientific method, but it was not an arid scientism; he left room for the play of ideas and even for "fantasy." He thought that dreams "should not run wild," that they "must be disciplined," but that dreams were important. He was speaking in more sober, less exuberant tones, but he had not yet developed that Olympian composure which the world would one day learn to identify with Lippmann. He was still a youthful seeker trying to find his way.

The intellectual tensions in *Drift and Mastery* reflect tensions within Lippmann himself. Despite his praise of spontaneity, he found it hard ever to relax his rigid control of his own feelings. Despite the humanistic strain in his writing, he found it difficult to cope with the real world and to mix with real people. One early acquaintance said bitterly to Mabel Dodge: "If you sometimes will go down to the Bowery and see the Booze victims, you will see another way in which God manifests himself. God doesn't manifest himself *at all* in Walter Lippmann." Mabel Dodge herself commented about her young companion: "Walter is never, never going to lose an eye in a fight. He might lose his glow, but he will never lose an eye." John Reed, who had known Lippmann since Harvard days, caught this element in a rather sorrowful poem about him:

> And with him LIPPMANN,—calm, inscrutable,
> Thinking and writing clearly, soundly, well;
> All snarls of falseness swiftly piercing through,
> His keen mind leaps like lightning to the True;
> His face is almost placid,—but his eye,—
> There is a vision born to prophecy!
> He sits in silence, as one who has said:
> "I waste not living words among the dead!"
> Our all-unchallenged Chief! But were there one
> Who builds a world, and leaves out all the fun,—
> Who dreams a pageant, gorgeous, infinite,
> And then leaves all the color out of it,—
> Who wants to make the human race, and me,
> March to a geometric Q.E.D.—
> Who but must laugh, if such a man there be?
> Who would not weep, if WALTER L. were he?

Drift and Mastery indicated that the issue was more in doubt than Reed implied. No one was asked to march to a geometric Q. E. D., and all the color had not been left out. Heinz Eulau, in a harsh but perceptive essay on Lippmann, has noted "the struggle in himself between the warm humanity which he sought and the abstract intellectualism which he feared." Yet it was a *struggle* and Lippmann did not surrender easily. Never was he able to think of himself as a man no more important than other men. Never could he involve himself deeply in the give and take of politics. Yet neither did he choose the easy alternative of a monkish withdrawal from the world of men. He remained a detached man who sought involvement. The tension that persisted within Lippmann, most readily apparent in *Drift and Mastery*, was to give value to his writings and his life.

August 1985   William E. Leuchtenburg

Introduction

In the early months of 1914 widespread unemployment gave the anarchists in New York City an unusual opportunity for agitation. The newspapers and the police became hysterical, men were clubbed and arrested on the slightest provocation, meetings were dispersed. The issue was shifted, of course, from unemployment to the elementary rights of free speech and assemblage. Then suddenly, the city administration, acting through a new police commissioner, took the matter in hand, suppressed official lawlessness, and guaranteed the men who were conducting the agitation their full rights.[1] This had a most disconcerting effect on the anarchists. They were suddenly stripped of all the dramatic effect that belongs to a clash with the police. They had to go back to the real issue of unemployment, and give some message to the men who had been following them. But they had no message to give: they knew what they were against but not what they were for, and their intellectual situation was as uncomfortable as one of those bad dreams in which you find yourself half-clothed in a public place.

Without a tyrant to attack an immature democracy is always somewhat bewildered. Yet we have to face the fact in America that what thwarts the growth of our civilization is not the uncanny, ma-

[1] Early in March 1914, the young radical Frank Tannenbaum led processions of the unemployed into New York's fashionable churches and insisted on shelter for the night. Tannenbaum's deeds and his subsequent trial, which resulted in his being sentenced to a year in prison, shook the world of New York intellectuals. Lippmann himself spoke at one mass meeting in Rutgers Square. It resulted in a number of demonstrations by anarchists and other groups which were handled sensibly by Mayor John Purroy Mitchel and his Police Commissioner, Douglas I. McKay.

licious contrivance of the plutocracy, but the faltering method, the distracted soul, and the murky vision of what we call grandiloquently the will of the people. If we flounder, it is not because the old order is strong, but because the new one is weak. Democracy is more than the absence of czars, more than freedom, more than equal opportunity. It is a way of life, a use of freedom, an embrace of opportunity. For republics do not come in when kings go out, the defeat of a propertied class is not followed by a coöperative commonwealth, the emancipation of woman is more than a struggle for rights. A servile community will have a master, if not a monarch, then a landlord or a boss, and no legal device will save it. A nation of uncritical drifters can change only the form of tyranny, for like Christian's sword, democracy is a weapon in the hands of those who have the courage and the skill to wield it; in all others it is a rusty piece of junk.

The issues that we face are very different from those of the last century and a half. The difference, I think, might be summed up roughly this way: those who went before inherited a conservatism and overthrew it; we inherit freedom, and have to use it. The sanctity of property, the patriarchal family, hereditary caste, the dogma of sin, obedience to authority,—the rock of ages, in brief, has been blasted for us. Those who are young to-day are born into a world in which the foundations of the older order survive only as habits or by default. So Americans can carry through their purposes when they have them. If the standpatter is still powerful amongst us it is because we have not learned to use our power, and direct it to fruitful ends. The American conservative, it seems to me, fills the vacuum where democratic purpose should be.

So far as we are concerned, then, the case is made out against absolutism, commercial oligarchy, and unquestioned creeds. *The rebel program is stated.* Scientific invention and blind social currents have made the old authority impossible in fact, the artillery fire of the iconoclasts has shattered its prestige. We inherit a rebel tradition. The dominant forces in our world are not the sacredness of property, nor the intellectual leadership of the priest; they are not the divinity of the constitution, the glory of industrial push, Victorian sentiment, New England respectability, the Republican Party, or John D. Rockefeller. Our time, of course, believes in change. The adjective "progressive" is what we like, and the word "new," be it the New Nationalism of Roosevelt, the New Freedom of Wilson, or the New Socialism of the syndicalists. The conservatives are more lonely than the pioneers, for almost any prophet to-day can have disciples. The leading thought of our world has ceased to regard commercialism either as permanent or desirable, and the only real question among intelligent people is how business methods are to be altered, not whether they are to be altered. For no one, unafflicted with invincible ignorance, desires to preserve our economic system in its existing form.

The business man has stepped down from his shrine; he is no longer an oracle whose opinion on religion, science, and education is listened to dumbly as the valuable by-product of a paying business. We have scotched the romance of success. In the emerging morality the husband is not regarded as the proprietor of his wife, nor the parents as autocrats over the children. We are met by women who are "emancipated"; for what we hardly know. We are not stifled by a classical tradition in art: in fact artists to-day are somewhat stunned by the rarefied atmosphere of their freedom. There is a wide agreement among thinking people that the body is not a filthy thing, and that to implant in a child the sense of sin is a poor preparation for a temperate life.

The battle for us, in short, does not lie against crusted prejudice, but against the chaos of a new freedom.

This chaos is our real problem. So if the younger critics are to meet the issues of their generation they must give their attention, not so much to the evils of authority, as to the weaknesses of democracy. But how is a man to go about doing such a task? He faces an enormously complicated world, full of stirring and confusion and ferment. He hears of movements and agitations, criticisms and reforms, knows people who are devoted to "causes," feels angry or hopeful at different times, goes to meetings, reads radical books, and accumulates a sense of uneasiness and pending change.

He can't, however, live with any meaning unless he formulates for himself a vision of what is to come out of the unrest. I have tried in this book to sketch such a vision for myself. At first thought it must seem an absurdly presumptuous task. But it is a task that everyone has to attempt if he is to take part in the work of his time.

For in so far as we can direct the future at all, we shall do it by laying what we see against what other people see. This doesn't mean the constructing of utopias. The kind of vision which will be fruitful to democratic life is one that is made out of latent promise in the actual world. There is a future contained in the trust and the union, the new status of women, and the moral texture of democracy. It is a future that can in a measure be foreseen and bent somewhat nearer to our hopes. A knowledge of it gives a sanction to our efforts, a part in a larger career, and an invaluable sense of our direction. We make our vision, and hold it ready for any amendment that experience suggests. It is not a fixed picture, a row of shiny ideals which we can exhibit to mankind, and say: Achieve these or be damned. All we can do is to search the world as we find it, extricate the forces that seem to move it, and surround them with criticism and suggestion. Such a vision will inevitably reveal the bias of its author; that is to say it will be a human hypothesis, not an oracular revelation. But if the hypothesis is honest and alive it should cast a little light upon our chaos. It should help us to cease revolving in the mere routine of the present or floating in a private utopia. For a vision of latent hope would be woven of vigorous strands; it would be concentrated on the crucial points of contemporary life, on that living zone where the present is passing into the future. It is the region where thought and action count. Too far ahead there is nothing but your dream; just behind, there is nothing but your memory. But in the unfolding present, man can be creative if his vision is gathered from the promise of actual things.

The day is past, I believe, when anybody can pretend to have laid down an inclusive or a final analysis of the democratic problem. Everyone is compelled to omit infinitely more than he can deal with; everyone is compelled to meet the fact that a democratic vision must be made by the progressive collaboration of many people. Thus I have touched upon the industrial problem at certain points that seem to me of outstanding importance, but there are vast sections and phases of industrial enterprise that pass unnoticed. The points I have raised are big in the world I happen to live in, but obviously they are not the whole world.

It is necessary, also, to inquire how "practical" you can be in a book of generalizations. That amounts to asking how detailed you can be. Well, it is impossible when you mention a minimum wage law, for example, to append a draft of the bill and a concrete set of rules for its administration. In human problems especially there is a vagueness which no one can escape entirely. Even the most voluminous study in three volumes of some legal question does not meet at every point the actual difficulties of the lawyer in a particular case. Generalization is always rough, and never entirely accurate. But it can be useful if it is made with a sense of responsibility to action. I have tried, therefore, to avoid gratuitously fine sentiments; I have tried to suggest nothing that with the information at my command doesn't seem at least probable.

This book, then, is an attempt to diagnose the current unrest and to arrive at some sense of what democracy implies. It begins with the obvious drift of our time and gropes for the conditions of mastery. I have tried in the essays that follow to enter the American problem at a few significant points in order to trace a little of the immense suggestion that radiates from them. I hope the book will leave the reader, as it does me, with a sense of the varied talents and opportunities, powers and organizations that may contribute to a conscious revolution. I have not been able to convince myself that one policy, one party, one class, or one set of tactics, is as fertile as human need.

It would be very easy if such a belief were possible. It would save time and energy and no end of grubbing: just to keep on repeating what you've learnt, eloquent, supremely confident, with the issues clean, a good fight and an inevitable triumph: Marx, or Lincoln, or Jefferson with you always as guide, counsellor and friend. All the thinking done by troubled dead men for the cocksure living; no class to consider but your own; no work that counts but yours; every party but your party composed of fools and rascals; only a formula to accept and a specific fight to win,—it would be easy. It might work on the moon.

Walter Lippmann
July 17, 1914.
46 East 80th Street,
New York City.

Part One

1

The Themes of Muckraking

There is in America to-day a distinct prejudice in favor of those who make the accusations. Thus if you announced that John D. Rockefeller was going to vote the Republican ticket it would be regarded at once as a triumph for the Democrats. Something has happened to our notions of success: no political party these days enjoys publishing the names of its campaign contributors, if those names belong to the pillars of society. The mere statement that George W. Perkins[1] is an active Progressive has put the whole party somewhat on the defensive. And there is more than sarcasm in the statement of the New York Times Annalist that:

"If it be true that the less bankers have to do with a scheme of banking and currency reform the more acceptable it will be to the people, it follows that the Administration's Currency Bill . . . must command popular admiration."

You have only to write an article about some piece of corruption in order to find yourself the target of innumerable correspondents, urging you to publish their wrongs. The sense of conspiracy and secret scheming which transpire is almost uncanny. "Big Business," and its ruthless tentacles, have become the material for the feverish fantasy of illiterate thousands thrown out of kilter

---

[1] George W. Perkins, a partner of J. P. Morgan and Company, helped found the Progressive Party of 1912, and was chosen chairman of its National Executive Committee. Although Perkins announced his support of the party's advanced social welfare platform, radicals in the party were highly suspicious of a "progressive" who had played a leading role in the formation of the International Harvester and Northern Securities combines.

by the rack and strain of modern life. It is possible to work yourself into a state where the world seems a conspiracy and your daily going is beset with an alert and tingling sense of labyrinthine evil. Everything askew—all the frictions of life are readily ascribed to a deliberate evil intelligence, and men like Morgan and Rockefeller take on attributes of omnipotence, that ten minutes of cold sanity would reduce to a barbarous myth. I know a socialist who seriously believes that the study of eugenics is a Wall Street scheme for sterilizing working-class leaders. And the cartoons which pictured Morgan sitting arrogantly in a chariot drawn by the American people in a harness of ticker tape,—these are not so much caricatures as pictures of what no end of fairly sane people believe. Not once but twenty times have I been told confidentially of a nation-wide scheme by financiers to suppress every radical and progressive periodical. But even though the most intelligent muckrakers have always insisted that the picture was absurd, it remains to this day a very widespread belief. I remember how often Lincoln Steffens used to deplore the frightened literalness with which some of his articles were taken. One day in the country he and I were walking the railroad track. The ties, of course, are not well spaced for an ordinary stride, and I complained about it. "You see," said Mr. Steffens with mock obviousness, "Morgan controls the New Haven and he prefers to make the people ride."

Now it is not very illuminating to say that this smear of suspicion has been worked up by the muckrakers. If business and politics really served American need, you could never induce people to believe so many accusations against them. It is said, also, that the muckrakers played for circulation, as if that proved their insincerity. But the mere fact that muckraking was what people wanted to hear is in many ways the most important revelation of the whole campaign.

There is no other way of explaining the quick approval which the muckrakers won. They weren't voices crying in a wilderness, or lonely prophets who were stoned. They demanded a hearing; it was granted. They asked for belief; they were believed. They cried that something should be done and there was every appearance of action. There must have been real causes for dissatisfaction, or the land notorious for its worship of success would not have turned so savagely upon those who had achieved it. A happy husband will endure almost anything, but an unhappy one is capable of flying into a rage if his carpet-slippers are not in the right place. For America, the willingness to believe the worst was a strange development in the face of its traditional optimism, a sign perhaps that the honeymoon was over. For muckraking flared up at about the time when land was no longer freely available and large scale industry had begun to throw vast questions across the horizon. It came when success had ceased to be easily possible for everyone. The muckrakers spoke to a public willing to recognize as corrupt an incredibly varied assortment of conventional acts. That is why there is nothing mysterious or romantic about the business of exposure,—no putting on of false hair, breaking into letter-files at midnight, hypnotizing financiers, or listening at keyholes. The stories of graft, written and unwritten, are literally innumerable. Often muckraking consists merely in dressing up a public document with rhetoric and pictures, translating a court record into journalese, or writing the complaints of a minority stockholder, a dislodged politician, or a boss gone "soft." No journalist need suffer from a want of material.

Now in writing this chapter I started out to visualize this material in systematic and scholarly fashion by making a list of the graft revelations in the last ten years. I wished for some quantitative sense of the number and kinds of act that are called corrupt. But I found myself trying to classify the industrial, financial, political, foreign and social relations of the United States, with hundreds of sub-heads, and a thousand gradations of credibility and exaggeration. It was an impossible task. The popular press of America is enormous, and for years it has been filled with "probes" and "amazing revelations." And how is a person to classify, say, the impeachment of a Tammany governor by a Tammany legislature? [2] A mere list of investigations would fill this book, and I abandoned the attempt with the mental reservation that if anyone really desired that kind of proof, a few German scholars, young and in perfect health, should be imported to furnish it.

They could draw up a picture to stagger even a jaded American.

[2] William Sulzer, who took office as Governor of New York in January 1913, was impeached and removed from office on October 18, 1913.

Suppose they began their encyclopedia with the adulteration of foods. There would follow a neat little volume on the aliases of coffee. The story of meat would help the vegetarians till the volume on canned foods appeared. Milk would curdle the blood, bread and butter would raise a scandal, candy,—the volume would have to be suppressed. If photographs could convey odors the study of restaurants might be done without words. The account of patent medicines, quack doctors, beauty parlors, mining schemes, loan sharks, shyster lawyers, all this riff-raff and fraud in the cesspool of commercialism would make unendurable reading. You would rush to the window, cursing the German pedants, grateful for a breath of that air which filters through in spite of the unenforced smoke ordinance of your city.

But the story would proceed. Think of your state of mind after you had read all about the methods of drummers, advertising agents, lobbyists, publicity men, after you knew adulteration of every description, and had learned the actual motives and history of political conferences, of caucuses, and consultations with the boss; suppose you understood the underground history of legislatures, the miscarriages of justice, the relations of the police to vice and crime, of newspapers to advertisers and wealthy citizens, of trade union leaders to their unions, the whole fetid story of the war between manufacturers and labor organizations. A study of the public domain in America would employ a staff of investigators. What railroads have done to the public, to their employees, what directors do to the stockholders and the property, the quantitative record of broken trust, the relation of bankers to the prosperity of business enterprise, of stock gamblers to capitalization,—taking merely all that is known and could be illustrated, summed up and seen at once, what a picture it would make.

And yet such a picture would be false and inept. For certainly there must be some ground for this sudden outburst of candor, some ground beside a national desire for abstract truth and righteousness. These charges and counter-charges arose because the world has been altered radically, not because Americans fell in love with honesty. If we condemn what we once honored, if we brand as criminal the conventional acts of twenty years ago, it's because we have developed new necessities and new expectations. They are the clue to the clouds of accusation which hang over American life. You cannot go very far by reiterating that public officials are corrupt, that business men break the law. The unbribed official and the law-abiding business man are not ideals that will hold the imagination very long. And that is why the earlier kind of muckraking exhausted itself. There came a time when the search for not-dishonest men ceased to be interesting. We all know now what tepid failures were those first opponents of corruption, the men whose only claim to distinction was that they had done no legal wrong. For without a vivid sense of what politics and business might be, you cannot wage a very fruitful campaign.

Now if you study the chief themes of muckraking I think it is possible to see the outlines of what America has come to expect.

The first wave of exposure insisted upon the dishonesty of politicians. Close upon it came widespread attack upon big business men, who were charged with bribing officials and ruining their competitors. Soon another theme appeared: big business men were accused of grafting upon the big corporations which they controlled. We are entering upon another period now; not alone big business, but all business and farming too, are being criticized for inefficiency, for poor product, and for exploitation of employees.

This classification is, of course, a very rough one. It would be easy enough to dispute it, for the details are endlessly complicated and the exceptions may appear very large to some people. But I think, nevertheless, that this classification does no essential violence to the facts. It doesn't matter for my purposes that some communities are still in what I call the first period, while others are in the third. For a nation like ours doesn't advance at the same rate everywhere. All I mean to suggest is that popular muckraking in the last decade has shifted its interest in something like this order: First, to the corruption of aldermen and mayors and public servants by the boss acting for a commercial interest, and to the business methods of those who built up the trusts. Then, muckraking turned, and began to talk about the milking of railroads by banks, and of one corporation by another. This period laid great emphasis on the "interlocking directorate." Now, muckraking is fastening upon the waste in management, upon working conditions as in the Steel Mills or at Lawrence,[3] or upon the quality of service rendered by the larger corporations. These have been the big themes.

Why should they have been? Why, to begin with, should politicians have been attacked so fiercely? Some people would say flatly: because politicians were dishonest. Yet that is an utterly unfounded generalization. The morals of politicians cannot by any stretch of the imagination be described as exceptionally bad. Politicians were on the make. To be sure. But who in this sunny land isn't? They gave their relatives and friends pleasant positions. What father doesn't do that for his son if he can, and with every feeling of righteousness? They helped their friends, they were loyal to those who had helped them: who will say that in private life these are not admirable virtues? And what were the typical grafts in politics—the grafts for which we tried to send politicians to jail? The city contracts for work, and the public official is in league with the contractor; but railroads also contract for work, and corporation officials are at least as frequently as politicians, financially interested in the wrong side of the deal. The city buys real estate, and the city official manages to buy it from himself or his friends. But railroad directors have been known to sell their property to the road they govern.

We can see, I think, what people meant by the word graft. They did not mean robbery. It is rather confused rhetoric to call a grafter a thief. His crime is not that he filches money from the safe but that he betrays a trust. The grafter is a man whose loyalty is divided and whose motives are mixed. A lawyer who takes a fee from both sides in some case; a public official who serves a private interest; a railroad director who is also a director in the supply

[3] In January 1912, a Congressional committee headed by Representative Augustus O. Stanley of Kentucky began a probe of U.S. Steel. At the hearings, Louis Brandeis disputed Judge Elbert Gary's claim that the firm practiced good labor relations and attacked the welfare plans of the company as "pensioned peonage." The strike of textile workers in Lawrence in 1912 captured the imagination of intellectuals. Originally spontaneous, the walkout was soon directed by IWW leaders who by their dramatic tactics aroused the concern of the nation over the plight of the mill workers. As part of the stirring "exodus of the children," some intellectuals took two hundred children of mill workers to New York to save them from violence or starvation.

company; a policeman in league with outlawed vice: those are the relationships which the American people denounce as "corrupt." The attempt to serve at the same time two antagonistic interests is what constitutes "corruption." The crime is serious in proportion to the degree of loyalty that we expect. A President of the United States who showed himself too friendly to some private interest would be denounced, though he may not have made one cent out of the friendship. But where we have not yet come to expect much loyalty we do very little muckraking. So if you inquired into the ethics of the buyer in almost any manufacturing house, you would find him doing things daily that would land the purchasing agent of a city in jail. Who regards it as especially corrupt if the selling firm "treats" the buyer, gives him or her a "present," perhaps a commission, or at least a "good time"? American life is saturated with the very relationship which in politics we call corrupt. The demand for a rake-off penetrates to the kitchen where a sophisticated cook expects a commission from the butcher, and tampers with the meat if it is refused; you can find it in the garage where the chauffeur has an understanding about the purchase of supplies; it extends to the golf caddie who regards a "lost" ball as his property and proceeds to sell it to the next man for half the original cost,—it extends to the man who buys that ball; and it ramifies into the professions when doctors receive commissions from specialists for sending patients to them; it saturates the work-a-day world with tips and fees and "putting you on to a good thing" and "letting you in on the ground floor." But in the politician it is mercilessly condemned.

That is because we expect more of the politician. We say in effect that no public servant must allow himself to follow the economic habits of his countrymen. The corrupt politician is he who brings into public service the traditions of a private career. Perhaps that is a cynical reflection. I do not know how to alter it. When I hear politicians talk "reform," I know they are advocating something which most drummers on the road would regard as the scruples of a prig, and I know that when business men in a smoking-room are frank, they are taking for granted acts which in a politician we should call criminal.

For the average American will condemn in an alderman what in his partner he would consider reason for opening a bottle of champagne. In literal truth the politician is attacked for displaying the morality of his constituents. You might if you didn't understand the current revolution, consider that hypocrisy. It isn't: it is one of the hopeful signs of the age. For it means that unconsciously men regard some of the interests of life as too important for the intrusion of commercial ethics.

Run a government to-day, with the same motives and vision that you run a dry goods store, and watch for the activity of the muckrakers. Pursue in the post office the methods which made you a founder of colleges, you will be grateful for a kind word from Mr. Lorimer.[4] Poor as they are, the standards of public life are so much more social than those of business that financiers who enter politics regard themselves as philanthropists. The amount of work and worry without reward is almost beyond the comprehension of the man whose every act is measured in profit and loss. The money to be accumulated in politics even by the cynically corrupt is so small by comparison that able men on the make go into politics only when their motives are mixed with ambition, a touch of idealism, vanity, or an imaginative notion of success.

But the fact that a public official took no bribe soon ceased to shield him from popular attack. Between the honest adherent of machine politics and the corruptionist himself the muckrakers made no sharp distinction. And that was because they had in a vague way come to expect positive action from men in office. They looked for better school systems, or health campaigns, or a conservation policy, that is for fairly concrete social measures, and officials who weren't for them were lumped together and denounced. The official might have read too much Adam Smith, or been too much of a lawyer, or taken orders from the boss, or a bribe from a lobbyist—the rough result was the same: he wasn't for what public opinion had come to expect, and the muckrakers laid their traps for him.

[4] George Horace Lorimer, editor of the *Saturday Evening Post*. Known in a later period as one of the most conservative journals in America, the *Post* in these years had a more liberal cast; in 1912 it had backed Roosevelt's Progressive Party.

I suppose that from the beginning of the republic people had always expected their officials to work at a level less self-seeking than that of ordinary life. So that corruption in politics could never be carried on with an entirely good conscience. But at the opening of this century, democratic people had begun to see much greater possibilities in the government than ever before. They looked to it as a protector from economic tyranny and as the dispenser of the prime institutions of democratic life.

But when they went to the government, what they found was a petty and partisan, slavish and blind, clumsy and rusty instrument for their expectations. That added to the violence of their attacks. When they had no vision of what a democratic state might do, it didn't make so very much difference if officials took a rake-off. The cost of corruption was only a little money, and perhaps the official's immortal soul. But when men's vision of government enlarged, then the cost of corruption and inefficiency rose: for they meant a blighting of the whole possibility of the state. There has always been corruption in American politics, but it didn't worry people very much, so long as the sphere of government was narrowly limited. Corruption became a real problem when reform through state action began to take hold of men's thought.

As muckraking developed, it began to apply the standards of public life to certain parts of the business world. Naturally the so-called public service corporation was the first to feel the pressure. There is obviously a great difference in outlook between the Vanderbilt policy of "the public be damned" and the McAdoo policy of "the public be pleased." [5] The old sense of private property is very much modified: few railroad men to-day would deny that they are conducting a quasi-public enterprise, and that something more is demanded of them than private exploitation. Thus President Mellen of the New Haven railroad could not have been handled more roughly by the people of New England if they

[5] Georgia-born William McAdoo had migrated to New York in the early 1890's. President of the Hudson and Manhattan Railroad Company, he had headed up the enterprise which tunneled the Hudson Tubes under the Hudson River. An enterprising businessman who was not identified with Wall Street, he had become the beau ideal businessman of the progressives by his slogan: "The public be pleased."

31

had elected him to office.[6] And his successor, President Howard Elliott, finds it necessary to remind the people that "the railroad is a public servant in fact as well as in name and that the service which it renders depends largely upon the treatment which it receives from its master." Mr. Elliott's grandfather would, I think, have said that his descendant lacked a sense of private property. That is true: Mr. Elliott's remark is a recognition that the cultural basis of property is radically altered, however much the law may lag behind in recognizing the change. So if the stockholders think they are the ultimate owners of the Pennsylvania railroad, they are colossally mistaken. Whatever the law may be, the people have no such notion. And the men who are connected with these essential properties cannot escape the fact that they are expected to act increasingly as public officials.

That expectation has filtered into the larger industrial corporations. I have here, for example, a statement by Roger Babson, a recognized financial expert:

"Suppose the mayor of a town should appoint his brother police commissioner; his daughter's husband, fire commissioner; his uncle, superintendent of the water works; and put his son in charge of the street cleaning department. How long would it be before the good citizens would hold an indignation meeting? It would not be long. No city in America would stand that kind of graft. Yet pick up the letterhead of a private corporation and what are you likely to find? It usually reads something like this: Quincy Persimmon, president; Quincy Persimmon, Jr., vice-president; Persimmon Quincy, treasurer; Howard Lemon, secretary. The presence of Howard Lemon in this select family circle is somewhat puzzling until one learns that Prunella Quincy Persimmon is the wife of Howard Lemon. Then all is clear. To be sure, the general manager of the concern, who is the man to see on any matter of special importance, is a man named Hobbs or Smith or Hogan,

---

[6] In August 1903, J. P. Morgan had picked Charles Sanger Mellen to head the New York, New Haven & Hartford Railroad Company. Mellen's management of the railroad aroused widespread opposition spearheaded by Louis Brandeis. In July 1913, after the road had been plagued by a series of serious accidents and rumors had spread that the road would soon be insolvent, a group of stockholders forced Mellen's resignation. In 1915, following an ICC inquiry which found malpractice in the railroad's operations, it went into receivership.

but it soon appears that the salary of the general manager is just about what it costs young Lemon to run his motor for one year . . . Has there ever been an American mayor who dared to run his city as this private corporation is run? In their leisure moments the Persimmons, Quincys and the Lemons are constantly advising their fellow citizens of the danger of permitting an American city to advance one step toward the sort of municipal work which is done by a great many foreign cities with success. The reason against this is given as the graft in public life." [7]

Now when the Persimmons are muckraked, what puzzles them beyond words is that anyone should presume to meddle with *their* business. What they will learn is that it is no longer altogether *their* business. The law may not have realized this, but the fact is being accomplished, and it's a fact grounded deeper than statutes. Big business men who are at all intelligent recognize this. They are talking more and more about their "responsibilities," their "stewardship." It is the swan-song of the old commercial profiteering and a dim recognition that the motives in business are undergoing a revolution.

But muckraking has grown in scope, which is another way of saying that it has come to expect still more. We hear now about the inefficiency of business. Men like Brandeis, Redfield, Taylor have taken the lead in this criticism.[8] Try if you can to imagine a merchant in the '70's subject to criticism on a national scale because he didn't know how to run his business. He would have sputtered and exploded at the impudence of such a suggestion. As a matter of fact some remnants of that age have sputtered and exploded at the impudence of Mr. Brandeis. But in the main the younger business men have been willing to listen. They do not think it a preposterous notion when the Secretary of Commerce suggests that if they are to conduct business they must do it efficiently. Then too, the farmers are being criticized. They are no longer deluged

---

[7] *Cleveland Press,* December 5, 1913. Quoted in *The Public,* December 26, 1913.

[8] The Boston attorney, Louis Brandeis, had charged that the trusts were not as efficient as smaller units. William Cox Redfield, a New York iron and steel manufacturer who sported side whiskers, had set forth his faith in scientific management in *The New Industrial Day* (New York: Century, 1912). Wilson later named him Secretary of Commerce. The father of scientific management was Frederic Winslow Taylor.

with adulation: they are being told quite frankly that they have a very great deal to learn from the government and the universities. And now there is a tremendous agitation about the quality of the goods and the conditions of labor under which they are produced.

Why all this has happened: why there are new standards for business men, why the nature of property is altered, why the workers and the purchasers are making new demands,—all this muckraking never made very clear. It was itself considerably more of an effect than a sign of leadership. It expressed a change, and consequently it is impossible to say that muckraking was either progressive or reactionary in its tendency. The attack upon business men was listened to by their defeated competitors as well as by those who looked forward to some better order of industrial life. Muckraking is full of the voices of the beaten, of the bewildered, and then again it is shot through with some fine anticipation. It has pointed to a revolution in business motives; it has hinted at the emerging power of labor and the consumer—we can take those suggestions, perhaps, and by analyzing them, and following them through, gather for ourselves some sense of what moves beneath the troubled surface of events.

2

New Incentives

We say in conversation: "Oh, no, he's not a business man, —he has a profession." That sounds like an invidious distinction, and no doubt there is a good deal of caste and snobbery in the sentiment. But that isn't all there is. We imagine that men enter the professions by undergoing a special discipline to develop a personal talent. So their lives seem more interesting, and their incentives more genuine. The business man may feel that the scientist content with a modest salary is an improvident ass. But he also feels some sense of inferiority in the scientist's presence. For at the bottom there is a difference of quality in their lives,—in the scientist's a dignity which the scramble for profit can never assume. The professions may be shot through with rigidity, intrigue, and hypocrisy: they have, nevertheless, a community of interest, a sense of craftsmanship, and a more permanent place in the larger reaches of the imagination. It is a very pervasive and subtle difference, but sensitive business men are aware of it. They are not entirely proud of their profit-motive: bankers cover it with a sense of importance, others mitigate it with charity and public work, a few dream of railroad empires and wildernesses tamed, and some reveal their sense of unworthiness by shouting with extra emphasis that they are not in business for their health.

It is a sharp commentary on the psychological insight of the orthodox economist who maintains that the only dependable motive is profit. Most people repeat that—parrot-fashion, but in the rub they don't act upon it. When we began to hear recently that radium might subdue cancer, there was a fairly unanimous demand that the small supply available should be taken over by the government and removed from the sphere of private exploitation. The fact is that men don't trust the profiteer in a crisis, or wherever the interest at stake is of essential importance. So the public regards a professor on the make as a charlatan, a doctor on the make as a quack, a woman on the make as an adventuress, a politician on the make as a grafter, a writer on the make as a hack, a preacher on the make as a hypocrite. For in science, art, politics, religion, the home, love, education,—the pure economic motive, profiteering, the incentive of business enterprise is treated as a public peril. Wherever civilization is seen to be in question, the Economic Man of commercial theorists is in disrepute.

I am not speaking in chorus with those sentimentalists who regard industry as sordid. They merely inherit an ancient and parasitic contempt for labor. I do not say for one instant that money is the root of evil, that rich men are less honest than poor, or any equivalent nonsense. I am simply trying to point out that there is in everyday life a widespread rebellion against the profit motive. That rebellion is not an attack on the creation of wealth. It is, on the contrary, a discovery that private commercialism is an antiquated, feeble, mean, and unimaginative way of dealing with the possibilities of modern industry.

The change is, I believe, working itself out under our very eyes. Each day brings innumerable plans for removing activities from the sphere of profit. Endowment, subsidy, state aid, endless varieties of consumers' and producers' coöperatives; public enterprise—they have been devised to save the theater, to save science and invention, education and journalism, the market basket and public utilities from the life-sapping direction of the commercialist. What is the meaning of these protean efforts to supersede the profiteer if not that his motive produces results hostile to use, and that he is a usurper where the craftsman, the inventor and the industrial statesman should govern? There is no sudden substitution of sacrifice for selfishness. These experiments are being tried because commercialism failed to serve civilization: the coöperator intrenched behind his wiser organization would smile if you regarded him as a patient lamb on the altar of altruism. He knows that the old economists were bad psychologists and superficial observers when they described man as a slot machine set in motion by inserting a coin.

It is often asserted that modern industry could never have been created had it not been given over to untrammeled exploitation by commercial adventurers. That may be true. There is no great point in discussing the question as to what might have happened if something else had happened in the past. Modern industry was created by the profiteer, and here it is, the great fact in our lives, blackening our cities, fed with the lives of children, a tyrant over men and women, turning out enormous stocks of produce, good, bad, and horrible. We need waste no time arguing whether any other motive could have done the work. What we are finding is that however effective profit may have been for inaugurating modern industry, it is failing as a method of realizing its promise. That is why men turned to coöperatives and labor unions; that is why the state is interfering more and more. These blundering efforts are the assertion of all the men and all those elements of their natures which commercialism has thwarted. No amount of argument can wipe out the fact that the profit-system has never commanded the whole-hearted assent of the people who lived under it. There has been a continuous effort to overthrow it. From Robert Owen to John Stuart Mill, from Ruskin through Morris to the varied radicalism of our day, from the millionaire with his peace palaces to Henry Ford with his generous profit-sharing, through the consumer organizing a coöperative market, to the workingmen defying their masters and the economists by pooling their labor, you find a deep stream of uneasiness, of human restlessness against those impositions which are supposed to rest on the eternal principles of man's being.

There is scarcely any need to press the point, for no one questions the statement that endowment, coöperation, or public enterprise are attempts to employ motives different from those of the profiteer. The only dispute is whether these new motives can be extended and made effective. It is, I think, a crucial question. It lies at the root of most theoretical objection to socialism in the famous "human nature" argument. Far from being a trivial question, as socialist debaters like to pretend,—it is the hardest nut they have to crack. They are proposing a reconstruction of human society, and in all honesty, they cannot dodge the question as to whether man as we know him is capable of what they ask. Persian, Mexican, Turkish and Chinese experience with constitutional democracies ought to show how easy it is, as Macaulay said, for a tailor to measure the clothes of all his customers by the Apollo Belvedere. In a matter like this there is little to choose between the socialist who is sure his plan will work and the "anti" who is sure it will not. The profit-motive is attacked, that is certain; that more or less successful attempts are made to supplant it, is obvious, but how far we can go, that remains an open question. We cannot answer it by analogy: it does not follow from the success of a coöperative grocery that the Steel Trust can be governed on the same plan. If our expectations are to have any solidity we must find evidence for them in those great private industries which seem to be completely in the hands of profit. That is where the issues join. The theater has always been a stamping ground for "queer" people; scholars are notoriously incompetent in "business"; scientific research pays so well, is so undeniably valuable, that few dare grudge it a subsidy; public utilities, like the highways, are by tradition not business propositions; and coöperatives have had a stormy history. There are, of course, the army and navy, which no man wishes to see organized by private individuals on the make. The most conservative have doubted recently whether armaments should be manufactured for profit. Yet such analogies, impressive as they are, offer nothing conclusive. But if we find that in the staple industries like steel and oil a silent revolution is in progress, then we have a basis for action. If there the profit-motive is decadent and new incentives ready, then perhaps what look like irresponsible outcries and wanton agitation will assume the dignity of a new morality.

In the last thirty years or so American business has been passing through a reorganization so radical that we are just beginning to grasp its meaning. At any rate for those of us who are young to-day the business world of our grandfathers is a piece of history that we can reconstruct only with the greatest difficulty. We know that the huge corporation, the integrated industry, production for a world market, the network of combinations, pools and agreements have played havoc with the older political economy. The scope of human endeavor is enormously larger, and with it has come, as Graham

Wallas says, a general change of social scale.[1] Human thought has had to enlarge its scale in order to meet the situation. That is why it is not very illuminating to say, for example, that the principles of righteousness are eternal and that the solution of every problem is in the Golden Rule. The Golden Rule in a village, and the Golden Rule for a nation of a hundred million people are two very different things. I might possibly treat my neighbor as myself, but in this vast modern world the greatest problem that confronts me is to find my neighbor and treat him at all. The size and intricacy which we have to deal with have done more than anything else, I imagine, to wreck the simple generalizations of our ancestors. After all, they were not prophets, and the conservative to-day makes an inhuman demand when he expects them to have laid out a business policy for a world they never even imagined. If anyone thinks that the Fathers might have done this let him sit down and write a political economy for the year 1950.

"Since the Sherman Act was passed (1890)," says President Van Hise of Wisconsin University, "a child born has attained its majority." Indeed he has, much to the surprise of the unwilling parents. Now a new business world has produced a new kind of business man. For it requires a different order of ability to conduct the Steel Trust, than it did to manage a primitive blast-furnace by means of a partnership. The giant corporation calls for an equipment unlike any that business has ever known: the minds of the managers are occupied with problems beyond the circle of ideas that interested the old-fashioned chop-whiskered merchants. They have to preserve intimate contact with physicists and chemists, there is probably a research laboratory attached to the plant. They have to deal with huge masses of workingmen becoming every day more articulate. They have to think about the kind of training our public schools give. They have to consider very concretely the psychology of races, they come into contact with the structure of credit, and a money

[1] See *The Great Society*, by Graham Wallas, for a psychological analysis of this change of social scale. I had the privilege of reading Mr. Wallas's book in manuscript while I was revising this one. My obligations go far deeper than that, however, for they extend back to the spring of 1910, when Mr. Wallas came from England to lecture at Harvard. In *A Preface to Politics* I tried to express my sense of the way in which Graham Wallas marks a turning point in the history of political thinking. —Walter Lippmann.

squeeze due to the Balkan war makes a difference in their rate of output. They have to keep thousands of ignorant stockholders somewhere in the back of their mind, people who don't know the difference between puddling and pudding. They may find themselves an issue in a political campaign, and if they are to be successful they must estimate correctly the social temper of the community. Diplomacy is closely related to the selling department, and perhaps at times they may have to dabble in Latin-American revolutions.

Mr. Louis D. Brandeis commented on this change of scale in his testimony before the Committee on Interstate Commerce.

"Anyone who critically analyzes a business learns this: that success or failure of an enterprise depends usually upon one man. . . . Now while organization has made it possible for the individual man to accomplish infinitely more than he could before, aided as he is by new methods of communication, by the stenographer, the telephone, and system, still there is a limit for what one man can do well . . . When, therefore, you increase your business to a very great extent, and the multitude of problems increases with its growth, you will find, in the first place, that the man at the head has a diminishing knowledge of the facts, and, in the second place, a diminishing opportunity of exercising careful judgment upon them."

In this statement, you will find, I believe, one of the essential reasons why a man of Mr. Brandeis's imaginative power has turned against the modern trust. He does not believe that men can deal efficiently with the scale upon which the modern business world is organized. He has said quite frankly, that economic size is in itself a danger to democracy. This means, I take it, that American voters are not intelligent enough or powerful enough to dominate great industrial organizations. So Mr. Brandeis, in company with many important thinkers the world over, has turned de-centralizer. The experience of history justifies his position in many respects: there is no doubt that an organization like the Holy Roman Empire was too large for the political capacity of human beings. It is probably true that the Morgan empire had become unwieldy. It may be that the Steel Trust is too large for efficiency. The splendid civilizations of the past have appeared in small cities. To-day if you go about the world you find that the small countries like Belgium, Holland, Denmark, are the ones that have come nearest to a high level of social prosperity. I once heard George Russell (Æ), the Irish poet and reformer, say that an ideal state would be about the size of County Cork.

Yet it is not very helpful to insist that size is a danger, unless you can specify what size.

The senators asked Mr. Brandeis that question. They pressed him to state approximately what percentage of an industry he considered an effective unit. He hesitated between ten per cent. and forty per cent., and could not commit himself. Obviously,—for how could Mr. Brandeis be expected to know? Adam Smith thought the corporations of his day doomed to failure on the very same grounds that Mr. Brandeis urges against the modern corporation. Now the million dollar organization is not too large for efficiency and the billion dollar one may be. The ideal unit may fall somewhere between? Where? That is a problem which experiments alone can decide, experiments conducted by experts in the new science of administration.

The development of that science is the only answer to the point Mr. Brandeis raises. Remarkable results have already been produced. Every one of us, for example, must wonder at times how the President of the United States ever does all the things the papers say he does. When, for example, does the man sleep? And is he omniscient? The fact is that administration is becoming an applied science, capable of devising executive methods for dealing with tremendous units. No doubt the President with his increasing responsibilities is an overworked man. No doubt there are trusts badly administered. No doubt there are inflated monopolies created for purely financial reasons. But just what the limits of administrative science are, a legislature is no more capable of determining than was Mr. Brandeis. Only experience, only trial and ingenuity, can demonstrate, and in a research so young and so swift in its progress, any effort to assign by law an arbitrary limit is surely the most obvious meddling. Say to-day that one unit of business is impossible, to-morrow you may be confronted with an undreamt success. Here if anywhere is a place where negative prophecy is futile. It is well to remember the classic case of that great scientist Simon Newcomb, who said that man would never fly. Two years before that statement was made, the Wright brothers had made secret flights. It may well be that the best unit is smaller than some of the modern trusts. It does not follow that we must break up industry into units of administration whose ideal efficiency is spent in competing with one another. I can understand, for example, the desire of many people to see Europe composed of a larger number of small nations. But I take it that everyone wishes these small nations to coöperate in the creation of a common European civilization. So it is with business. The unit of administration may be whatever efficiency demands. It may be that the steel industry would gain if it were conducted by forty corporations. But at the same time there are advantages in common action which we cannot afford to abandon. Technical improvement must be for the whole industry, the labor market must be organized and made stable, output must be adjusted to a common plan. The appearance of federal organization seems to suggest a possible compromise in which the administrative need for decentralization is combined with the social demand for a unified industrial policy.

No one, surely, proposes to revive the little business monarch who brooded watchfully over every operation in factory and office, called his workingmen by their pet names, and was impelled at almost every turn by Adam Smith's "natural propensity to truck and barter." For just as in political government "the President" does a hundred things every day he may never even hear of, just as the English Crown acts constantly through some unknown civil servant at $1,500 a year,—so in big business,—the real government is passing into a hierarchy of managers and deputies, who, by what would look like a miracle to Adam Smith, are able to coöperate pretty well toward a common end. They are doing that, remember, in the first generation of administrative science. They come to it unprepared, from a nation that is suspicious and grudging. They have no tradition to work with, the old commercial morality of the exploiter and profiteer still surrounds these new rulers of industry. Perhaps they are unaware that they are revolutionizing the discipline, the incentives, and the vision of the business world. They do brutal and stupid things, and their essential work is obscured. But they are conducting business on a scale without precedent in history.

The real news about business, it seems to me, is that it is being administered by men who are not profiteers. The managers are on salary, divorced from ownership and from bargaining. They represent the revolution in business incentives at its very heart. For they conduct gigantic enterprises and they stand outside the higgling of the market, outside the shrewdness and strategy of competition. The motive of profit is not their personal motive. That is an astounding change. The administration of the great industries is passing into the hands of men who cannot halt before each transaction and ask themselves: what is my duty as the Economic Man looking for immediate gain? They have to live on their salaries, and hope for promotion, but their day's work is not measured in profit. There are thousands of these men, each with responsibilities vaster than the patriarchs of industry they have supplanted. It is for the commercial theorists to prove that the "ability" is inferior, and talent less available.

It is no accident that the universities have begun to create graduate schools of business-administration. Fifty years ago industry was an adventure or perhaps a family tradition. But to-day it is becoming a profession with university standing equal to that of law, medicine, or engineering. The universities are supplying a demand. It is big business, I believe, which has created that demand. For it is no longer possible to deal with the present scale of industry if your only equipment is what men used to call "experience," that is, a haphazard absorption of knowledge through the pores. Just as it is no longer possible to become a physician by living with doctors, just as law cannot be grasped by starting as a clerk in some attorney's office, so business requires a greater preparation than a man can get by being a bright, observant, studious, ambitious office boy, who saves his money and is good to his mother.

What it will mean to have business administered by men with a professional training is a rather difficult speculation. That it is a very far-reaching psychological change, I have no doubt. The professions bring with them a fellowship in interest, a standard of ethics, an esprit de corps, and a decided discipline. They break up that sense of sullen privacy which made the old-fashioned business man so impervious to new facts and so shockingly ignorant of the larger demands of civilized life. I know that the professions develop their pedantry, but who was ever more finicky, more rigid in his thinking than the self-satisfied merchant? It would be idle to suppose that we are going suddenly to develop a nation of reasonable men. But at least we are going to have an increasing number of "practical" men who have come in contact with the scientific method. That is an enormous gain over the older manufacturers and merchants. They were shrewd, hard-working, no doubt, but they were fundamentally uneducated. They had no discipline for making wisdom out of their experience. They had almost no imaginative training to soften their primitive ambitions. But doctors and engineers and professional men, generally, have something more than a desire to accumulate and outshine their neighbors. They have found an interest in the actual work they are doing. The work itself is in a measure its own reward. The instincts of workmanship, of control over brute things, the desire for order, the satisfaction of services rendered and uses created, the civilizing passions are given a chance to temper the primal desire to have and to hold and to conquer.

3

The Magic of Property

The ordinary editorial writer is a strong believer in what he calls the sanctity of private property. But as far as highly organized business is concerned he is a pilgrim to an empty shrine. The trust movement is doing what no conspirator or revolutionist could ever do: it is sucking the life out of private property. For the purposes of modern industry the traditional notions have become meaningless: the name continues, but the fact is disappearing. You cannot conduct the great industries and preserve intact the principles of private property. And so the trusts are organizing private property out of existence, are altering its nature so radically that very little remains but the title and the ancient theory.

When a man buys stock in some large corporation he becomes in theory one of its owners. He is supposed to be exercising his instinct of private property. But how in fact does he exercise that instinct which we are told is the only real force in civilization? He may never see *his* property. He may not know where his property is situated. He is not consulted as to its management. He would be utterly incapable of advice if he were consulted. Contact with *his* property is limited to reading in the newspapers what it is worth each day, and hoping that dividends will be paid. The processes which make him rich in the morning and poor in the evening, increase his income or decrease it,—are inscrutable mysteries. Compare him with the farmer who owns his land, the homesteader or the prospector, compare him with anyone who has a real sense of possession, and you will find, I think, that the modern shareholder is a very feeble representative of the institution of private property. No one has ever had a more abstract relation to the thing he owned. The absentee landlord is one of the sinister figures of history. But the modern shareholder is not only an absentee, he is a transient too. The week ending January 10, 1914, was generally regarded as a dull one in Wall Street. Yet on the New York Stock Exchange alone the total sales amounted to 1,777,038 shares. About 340,000 shares of private property in Reading changed hands.

With a few thousand dollars I can be an owner in Massachusetts textile mills on Monday, in Union Pacific on Tuesday. I can flit like a butterfly from industry to industry. I don't even have to use my judgment as to where I shall alight. All I have to do is to choose some well-known stock broker and put myself into his hands. And when I read in books on political economy that any profit I make is a reward for my foresight, my courage in the face of risk, I laugh. I know that I can't have any foresight. I don't understand the inner workings of the business world. I'm not allowed to know. That is reserved for specialists like stock brokers and private bankers. In the modern world investing has become a highly skilled profession, altogether beyond the capacities of the ordinary shareholder. The great mass of people who have saved a little money can no more deal with their property on their own initiative than they can deal with disease or war on their own initiative. They have to act through representatives. Just as they need physicians and organized armies, so they have to have stock brokers, financial experts, public service commissions and the rest.

There has been in recent years a great outcry against the concentrated control of credit. It was found that the decision as to how money should be invested had passed away from the people who owned the money. The enormous power of Morgan consisted in his ability to direct the flow of capital. He was the head of a vast system which had taken out of the hands of investors the task of deciding how their money was to be used. It was no doubt a colossal autocracy. There has been a great effort to break it up, to decentralize the power that concentrated about Morgan. But no one proposes to put back into the hands of the investor the decision as to the financing of industry. The investors are a scattered mob incapable of such decisions. The question of where money is to be applied is a matter for experts to answer. And so reform of the credit system does not consist in abolishing the financial expert. It consists in making him a public servant. The Wilson Currency Bill [1] seems to be an effort to make banking responsive to business needs all over the country. It gives business men a larger control over financial experts. How that control is to be extended to the citizens at large is one of the subtlest problems of democracy. I do not venture here to answer it. I wish rather to keep more closely to the fact that whatever system is devised, it will have to recognize that the investor no longer can decide in modern industry, that "foresight" has become an organized, technical profession, and is ceasing to be one of the duties of private property.

Not long ago the Interstate Commerce Commission gave a very neat recognition to this change. It issued a report on the bankruptcy of the Frisco railway which contained a condemnation of certain private bankers for offering bonds to the investing public when the bankers should have known that the road was insolvent. The Commission was saying that the investor couldn't know, that he was in the hands of experts, and that the experts have a trust to perform. You couldn't very well go to greater lengths in announcing the impotence of private property. For where in the name of sanity have all the courage, foresight, initiative gone to, what has happened to all the rugged virtues that are supposed to be inherent in the magic of property?

They have gone a-glimmering with the revolutionary change that the great industry has produced. Those personal virtues belong to an earlier age when men really had some personal contact with their property. But to-day the central condition of business is that capital shall be impersonal, "liquid," "mobile." The modern shareholder as a person is of no account whatever. It mattered very much what kind of people the old landlords were. But it matters not at all what kind of person the shareholder is. He may be ignorant or wise, he may be a child in arms or a greybeard in his dotage, he may live in Iceland or Patagonia: he has no genuine rôle in the conduct of in-

[1] On June 26, 1913, Representative Carter Glass of Virginia and Senator Robert L. Owen of Oklahoma introduced a revised banking and currency bill which was adopted as the Federal Reserve Act on December 23, 1913.

dustry. He cannot fulfil any responsibility to the property he owns. That is why it is so futile to attack clergymen and reformers whc happen to own stock in some ruthless factory. They have no real power to alter the situation.

You often hear it said that the stockholders must be made to realize their duties. Not long ago, for example, when the wretched working conditions of the Steel Mills were exposed, a very well-meaning minority stockholder did protest and cause a slight flurry in the newspapers. But the notion that the 200,000 owners of the Steel Trust can ever be aroused to energetic, public-spirited control of "their" property—that is as fantastic as anything that ever issued from the brain of a lazy moralist. Scattered all over the globe, changing from day to day, the shareholders are the most incompetent constituency conceivable. Think how difficult it is to make the voters in one town exhibit any capacity for their task. Well, the voters in the government of the Steel Trust do not meet each other every day, do not read the same newspapers: the suffrage qualifications for the Steel Trust have nothing to do with age, sex, nationality, residence, literacy; the one qualification is the possession of some money and the desire for more. Shareholders are a heterogeneous collection with a single motive, and from that material some people pretend to expect a high sense of social responsibility.

I do not mean to imply, of course, that because a man owns stock he is necessarily ignorant or tyrannical. He may be as benevolent as you please. But the fact that he owns stock will not enable him to practice his benevolence. He will have to find other ways of expressing it. For shareholding in the modern world is not adapted to the exercise of any civilizing passion. It is too abstract, too scattered, too fluctuating.

All this is a natural result of the largescale corporation. In the partnership and firm, owners and managers are in general the same people, but the corporation has separated ownership from management. Ownership has been opened to a far larger number of people than it ever was before, and it means less than it used to. Each stockholder owns a smaller share in a far greater whole. The trusts have concentrated control and management, but ownership they have diffused and diluted till it means very little more than a claim to residual profits, after expenses are paid, after the bondholders are satisfied, and perhaps, after the insiders have decided which way they wish the stock market to fluctuate.

Let no stockholder come to the radical, then, and charge him with attacking the sanctity of private property. The evolution of business is doing that at a rate and with a dispatch which will make future historians gasp. If the reformers should, for example, arrive at the point of deciding to abolish private property in railroads, they would discover that most of the rights of property had already disappeared. Management has long ago passed out of the hands of the stockholders; the right to fix rates has been absorbed by the state; the right to fix wages is conditioned by very powerful unions. They would find stockholding in the last stages of decay, where not even the dividends were certain. And one of the most difficult problems reformers may have to face will be the eagerness of railroad owners to give up the few vestiges of private property which are left to them, if they can secure instead government bonds. They may feel far happier as creditors of the United States than as representatives of the institution of private property.

Government ownership will probably be a very good bargain for railroad stockholders. To-day they are a little less than creditors; they loan their money, and they are not sure of a return. Government ownership may make them real creditors—that is the highest hope which remains from the shattered glamour that came from the magic of property.

What has happened to the railroads is merely a demonstration of what is likely to happen to the other great industries—steel, oil, lumber, coal and all the others which are adapted to large scale production. Private property will melt away; its functions will be taken over by the salaried men who direct them, by government commissions, by developing labor unions. The stockholders deprived of their property rights are being transformed into money-lenders.

It is evident that the question of nationalizing industries is not a choice between the maintenance of private property and its abolition. In amateur socialist discussions this is always made the issue whenever someone proposes to substitute public operation for private. It betrays an unreal sense of the problem. There is no very essential difference between holding the securities of the Steel Trust and those of the U.S. Government. The government bonds are, if anything, a more certain investment. But there is some difference between public and private enterprise: what is it?

Opponents of collectivism argue that government work is inefficient. They seem to imply that the alleged superiority of private management is due to the institution of private property. That, it seems to me, is a striking example of what logicians call false cause. If the Steel Trust is efficient, it is not due to the existence of its 200,000 stockholders. It is due to the fact that the management is autocratic, that administrators are highly paid, and given power adequate to their responsibility. When governments are willing to pursue that course, they can be just as efficient as private management. The construction of the Panama Canal is a classic example of what government can do if it is ready to centralize power and let it work without democratic interruption.

The real problem of collectivism is the difficulty of combining popular control with administrative power. Private property is no part of the issue. For any industry which was ready for collectivism would have abolished private property before the question arose. What would remain for discussion would be the conflict between democracy and centralized authority. That is the line upon which the problems of collectivism will be fought out—how much power shall be given to the employees, how much to the ultimate consumer, how much to sectional interests, how much to national ones. Anyone who has watched the disillusionment of labor with the earlier socialism and has understood the meaning of the syndicalist trend will know how radically the real difficulties of public enterprise differ from those presented in theoretical debates.

I do not wish at this point to draw any conclusion as to the solution of the trust problem. I am trying to sketch very roughly the main elements in the actual situation. The incentive of the men who conduct modern industry was the first point of interest. It is obvious that the trusts have created a demand for a new type of business man—for a man whose motives resemble those of the applied scientist and whose responsibility is that of a public servant. Nothing would be easier than to shout for joy, and say that everything is about to be fine: the business men are undergoing a change of heart. That is just what an endless number of American reformers are shouting, and their prophet is Gerald Stanley Lee.[2] The notion seems to be that workers, politicians, consumers and the rest are to have no real part in the glorious revolution which is to be consummated for their benefit. It is not hard to understand the habit of mind which leads men to these conclusions. The modern world is brain-splitting in its complexity, and if you succeed in disentangling from it some hopeful trend there is nothing more restful than to call it the solution of the problem. Those who have seen the change in business motives have, I believe, good ground for rejoicing, but they might in decency refrain from erecting upon it a mystic and rhetorical commercialism.

For the same reason, it is well not to take too literally the revolution in private property. This revolution has not happened to all property. It is most advanced in the railroads and what we call public service corporations. It is imminent in the big staple industries which are adapted to large scale production. But there remains a vast amount of genuine private property in agricultural land, in competitive business.

In the great industries themselves, however, it is important to notice that with the diminishing importance of ownership, the control has passed for the time being into the hands of investment experts, the banking interests. That control is challenged now, not by the decadent stockholders, but by those most interested in the methods of industry: the consumer, the worker, and the citizen at large.

[2] One of the earliest of the public relations men, Lee wrote *Inspired Millionaires* in 1908.

4

Caveat Emptor

I am sure that few consumers feel any of that sense of power which economists say is theirs. No doubt when Mr. Morgan was buying antiques there came to him a real sense that he commanded the market. But the ordinary man with a small income to spend is much more like a person who becomes attached to an energetic bulldog, and leaves the spectators wondering which is the mover and which the moved. He is the theoretical master of that dog. . . .

The consumer is sometimes represented as the person whose desires govern industry. Actually, he is an ignorant person who buys in the dark. He takes what he can get at the price he can afford. He is told what he wants, and then he wants it. He rides in a packed subway because he has to, and he buys a certain kind of soap because it has been thrust upon his soul. Where there is a monopoly the consumer is, of course, helpless, and where there is competition he is almost entirely at the mercy of advertising.

Advertising, in fact, is the effort of business men to take charge of consumption as well as production. They are not content to supply a demand, as the text-books say; they educate the demand as well. In the end, advertising rests upon the fact that consumers are a fickle and superstitious mob, incapable of any real judgment as to what it wants or how it is to get what it thinks it would like. A bewildered child in a toy shop is nothing to the ultimate consumer in the world market of to-day. To say, then, that advertising is merely a way of calling attention to useful goods is a gorgeous piece of idealization. Advertising is in fact the weed that has grown up because the art of consumption is uncultivated. By advertising I don't mean descriptive catalogues which enable the buyer to select. I mean the deceptive clamor that disfigures the scenery, covers fences, plasters the city, and blinks and winks at you through the night. When you contemplate the eastern sky ablaze with chewing gum, the northern with tooth-brushes and underwear, the western with whiskey, and the southern with petticoats, the whole heavens brilliant with monstrously flirtatious women, when you glance at magazines in which a rivulet of text trickles through meadows of automobiles, baking powders, corsets and kodaks, you begin to accumulate a sense of the disastrous incompetence of the ultimate consumer.

For the scale on which the world is organized to-day discrimination has become impossible for the ordinary purchaser. He hasn't time to candle every egg he buys, test the milk, inquire into the origins of the meat, analyze the canned food, distinguish the shoddy, find out whether the newspapers are lying, avoid meretricious plays, and choose only railroads equipped with safety devices. These things have to be done for him by experts backed with authority to enforce their decisions. In our intricate civilization the purchaser can't pit himself against the producer, for he lacks knowledge and power to make the bargain a fair one. By the time goods are ready for the ultimate consumer they have travelled hundreds of miles, passed through any number of wholesalers, jobbers, middlemen and what not. The simple act of buying has become a vast, impersonal thing which the ordinary man is quite incapable of performing without all sorts of organized aid. There are silly anarchists who talk as if such organization were a loss of freedom. They seem to imagine that they can "stand alone," and judge each thing for themselves. They might try it. They would find that the purchase of eggs was such a stupendous task that no time would be left over for the purchase of beer or the pursuit of those higher freedoms for which they are fighting.

The old commercial theorists had some inkling of these difficulties. They knew that the consumer could not possibly make each purchase a deliberate and intelligent act. So they said that if only business men were left to compete they would stumble over each other to supply the consumer with the most satisfactory goods. It is hardly necessary to point out how complete has been the collapse of that romantic theory. There are a hundred ways of competing, to produce the highest quality at the lowest cost proved to be the most troublesome and least rewarding form of competition. To cheapen the quality, subtract value that does not appear on the surface, lower the standards of workmanship, to adulterate, in short, was a more "natural" method of competition than the noble Platonic method which economists talked about. And then came price agreements, the elimination of "cut-throat" competition, and the consumer began to realize that he couldn't trust to the naïve notions of the nineteenth century.

He turned to the government for aid, and out of that has grown a fresh sense of the uses of politics. The old commercialists saw in government little more than the police power; the modern syndicalists refuse to believe that the state can be anything but an agent of tyranny. But the facts belie both notions. Politics is becoming the chief method by which the consumer enforces his interests upon the industrial system.

Many radical socialists pretend to regard the consumer's interest as a rather mythical one. "All the people" sounds so sentimental, so far removed from the clash of actual events. But we are finding, I think, that the real power emerging to-day in democratic politics is just the mass of people who are crying out against the "high cost of living." That is a consumer's cry. Far from being an impotent one, it is, I believe, destined to be stronger than the interests either of labor or of capital. With the consumer awake, neither the worker nor the employer can use politics for his special interest. The public, which is more numerous than either side, is coming to be the determining force in government.

Votes for women will increase the power of the consumer enormously. The mass of women do not look at the world as workers; in America, at least their prime interest is as consumers. It is they who go to market and do the shopping; it is they who have to make the family budget go around; it is they who feel shabbiness and fraud and high prices most directly. They have more time for politics than men, and it is no idle speculation to say that their influence will make the consumer the real master of the political situation.

It is through government that people are seeking to impose upon business a maximum of quality and a minimum of cost. Price fixing is already in operation for public utilities; there is every reason to believe that it will be extended to the great industries. The amount of inspecting of products which is already being done it is impossible to record. I don't say that it is effective or satisfactory, but it is a force to be reckoned with and it is sure to grow. We hear a great deal about the class-consciousness of labor; my own observation is that in America to-day consumers'-consciousness is growing very much faster.

What forms it will assume with time is not easy to predict. The great extension of collectivism which is at hand will be carried through and dominated by the "public." The workers will have very little to say about it, as workers. The public is capable of oppression, I have no doubt, and when I say that consumers are going to dominate the government I do not state the fact with unmixed joy. There will be a tyranny of the majority for which minorities will have to prepare. But good or bad, collectivism or "state socialism" is perhaps the chief instrument of the awakened consumer.

One of the heritages from competitive business was almost complete disorganization in selling of wares. Six grocers in three blocks, dingy little butcher-shops, little retail businesses with the family living in the back room, the odor of cooking to greet you as you enter the door, fly-specks on the goods—walk through any city and marvel at the anarchy of retail business. Well, the large department store, organized markets, the chain of stores, the mail order business, are changing the situation radically for the purchaser.

They are focussing his attention: he could not focus on a congery of little shops. But where there is centralization, he has something of which to take hold. The solidarity of the consumer is made possible, just as large scale production is making possible a much greater solidarity for labor. But it is doubtful whether the public will be satisfied to stand outside these large retail organizations, and try to regulate them through government inspectors. The example of the English Coöperative Societies is very attractive. They represent a power for the consumer, and in the face of the high cost of living, the consumer is looking for power.

Business, then, must look forward to increasing control in the

55

interests of those who buy. Processes will be inspected, and regulated by law, some industries will be operated directly by the government, and producers in general may face coöperative organizations grown powerful enough perhaps to command the market. Those seem to be the general methods by which the consumer is trying to redeem his helplessness in the complexity of the newly organized industrial world.

It is interesting to notice the revolutionary standards which are being generated by this young social power. Take the matter of prices. That, after all, is the first item that interests the purchaser. Quality is a subtler notion. But in the matter of prices, there is coming into existence an idea that profits can be "unreasonable." It is an idea that runs counter to the whole fabric of the old commercialism, where the only recognized motive was profit and the only ideal all that the traffic would bear. To talk about "reasonable returns" is to begin an attack on industrialism which will lead far beyond the present imaginations of the people who talk about it. The whole question of unearned wealth is opened up, for "unreasonable" profit can mean only unearned profit. Just where those words lead nobody seems to know. But there is a groping behind them which points without question to a radical attack on large incomes. The consumer talks about "reasonable return" because he feels that any profit which keeps prices high must be unreasonable. That may seem a curious logic, but it's the kind of logic which half-conscious democracies use.

5

A Key to the Labor Movement

When employers talk about the freedom of labor, it may be that some of them are really worried over the hostility of most unions to exceptional rewards for exceptional workers. But in the main that isn't what worries them. They are worried about their own freedom, not the freedom of wage-earners. They dislike the union because it challenges their supremacy. And they fight unions as monarchs fight constitutions, as aristocracies fight the vote. When an employer tells about his own virtues, he dilates upon his kindness, his fairness, and all the good things he has done for his men. That is just what benevolent autocrats do: they try to justify their autocracy by their benevolence. Indeed, the highest vision of those who oppose unions is that the employer will develop the virtues of a good aristocrat.

But, of course, wage-earners are not dealing with men inspired by a sense of *noblesse* or *richesse oblige*. Henry Ford is a sensational rarity among employers.[1] No doubt there are some others, not so conspicuous. Now, if workers faced only men with such an outlook, I don't think their problem would be solved, but it would take on a very different complexion. This is, however, an academic question, for the great mass of employers show no desire to make big concessions.

Employers are organized for obstruction. There is, for ex-

[1] Although to a later generation Herny Ford was known as a bitter foe of unionism, in these years he was regarded as a model employer because of his well-publicized high wage policy and profit-sharing plans.

ample, the National Association of Manufacturers, embracing four thousand individual employers, who represent a capital of about ten billion dollars. Their constructive program consists of such attractive items as "unalterable antagonism to the closed shop," opposition to eight-hours' bills, and with mild emphasis hostility "to any and all anti-injunction bills of whatever kind." American civilization is also assisted by the National Council for Industrial Defense, an unincorporated body which employs a lobbyist at the rate of a thousand dollars a month. According to the proud words of its late President, this Council "in the number of members, in the capital which they control, and in the social, industrial and political influence which they exert . . . is by far the largest and most powerful league of conservative and public-spirited citizens ever formed in any country of the world." [2]

There are also a number of national associations in various trades endeavoring to prevent wage-earners from submerging their individuality in unions. They have been known to refuse advertising to papers which were friendly to organized labor—on the highest grounds, of course, such high grounds being a refusal "to pander to the unthrifty class." They have been known to use the black-list, though of course they do not approve of it. They have been known to place spies in labor unions to protect workers against themselves. They have been known to use what revolutionists call the "provocateur": in Cleveland during the garment strike there was a glib, plausible person who talked dynamite in an effort to discredit the union. There have been some actual "planting" of dynamite as at Lawrence, a little beating up as at Calumet, kidnapping, private armies, gatling guns and armored trains as at West Virginia and Colorado.[3]

[2] Harry W. Laidler, *Boycotts and the Labor Struggle* (New York: John Lane, 1914). The President of the National Council for Industrial Defense was James W. Van Cleave.

[3] The copper strike of the Western Federation of Miners in Calumet was one of the most violent in the country. In the Kanawha valley of West Virginia, striking United Mine Workers engaged in a bloody civil war with mine guards. Mother Jones, the "Stormy Petrel of Labor," was imprisoned in this fight to unionize all the coal fields of West Virginia. At Ludlow, Colorado a strike against the Rockefeller-controlled Colorado Fuel and Iron Company had ended in the "Ludlow massacre." Militia and mine guards had turned machine guns on the tent colony of striking coal miners and set the tents afire; women and children died in the flames.

It is well known, of course, that newspapers make every effort to enable workingmen to reach public opinion, and make their appeal not to force but to the national conscience. All civil rights are carefully guarded for workers as in Paterson,[4] Lawrence, and the southern lumber camps. Employers are precise in their desire to secure judges who have no bias whatever. And the voters are an active, intelligent body of imaginative democrats fighting at every step to see that justice is done.

The fact is that nothing is so stubbornly resisted as the attempt to organize labor into effective unions. Yet it is labor organized that alone can stand between America and the creation of a permanent, servile class. Unless labor is powerful enough to be respected, it is doomed to a degrading servitude. Without unions no such power is possible. Without unions industrial democracy is unthinkable. Without democracy in industry, that is where it counts most, there is no such thing as democracy in America. For only through the union can the wage-earner participate in the control of industry, and only through the union can he obtain the discipline needed for self-government. Those who fight unions may think they are fighting its obvious errors, but what they are really against is just this encroachment of democracy upon business.

Now men don't agitate for democracy because it is a fine theory. They come to desire it because they have to, because absolutism does not work out any longer to civilized ends. Employers are not wise enough to govern their men with unlimited power, and not generous enough to be trusted with autocracy. That is the plain fact of the situation: the essential reason why private industry has got to prepare itself for democratic control.

I don't pretend for one moment that labor unions are far-seeing, intelligent, or wise in their tactics. I have never seen a political democracy that aroused uncritical enthusiasm. It seems to me simply that the effort to build up unions is as much the work of pioneers, as the extension of civilization into the wilderness. The unions are the first feeble effort to conquer the industrial jungle

[4] Violence had been employed to help break the Paterson textile strike. On June 7, 1913, intellectuals staged the famous Paterson pageant: thousands of strikers marched to Madison Square Garden behind an I.W.W. band; inside the Garden, the strikers re-enacted episodes of the strike including the funeral of a worker killed by the police.

for democratic life. They may not succeed, but if they don't their failure will be a tragedy for civilization, a loss of cooperative effort, a baulking of energy, and the fixing in American life of a class-structure.

The unions are struggling where life is nakedly brutal, where the dealings of men have not been raised even to the level of discussion which we find in politics. There is almost as little civil procedure in industry as there is in Mexico, or as there was on the American frontier. To expect unionists then to talk with velvet language, and act with the deliberation of a college faculty is to be a tenderfoot, a victim of your class tradition. The virtues of labor to-day are frontier virtues, its struggles are for rights and privileges that the rest of us inherited from our unrefined ancestors.

Men are fighting for the beginnings of industrial self-government. If the world were wise that fight would be made easier for them. But it is not wise. Few of us care for ten minutes in a month about these beginnings or what they promise. And so the burden falls entirely upon the workers who are directly concerned. They have got to win civilization, they have got to take up the task of fastening a worker's control upon business.

No wonder they despise the scab. He is justly despised. Far from being the independent, liberty-loving soul he is sometimes painted, the scab is a traitor to the economic foundations of democracy.[5] He makes the basic associations of men difficult. He is an indigestible lump in the common life, and it is he who generates nine-tenths of the violence in labor disputes. Democracies of workingmen have to fight him out of sheer self-protection, as a nation has to fight a mutiny, as doctors have to fight a quack. The clubbing of scabs is not a pretty thing; the importation of scabs is an uglier one. It is perhaps true that there is, as ex-President Eliot said, no such thing as peaceful picketing. There is no such thing as a peaceful coast defense or a gentlemanly border patrol. The picket-line is to these little economic democracies the guardian of their integrity, their chief protection from foreign invasion.

Without some security no internal growth is possible. As long as the unions have to fight for mere existence, their immense con-

[5] Charles W. Eliot, the president of Harvard University, had called the scab a type of modern hero.

structive possibilities will be obscured in the desperation of the struggle. The strike-breaker, then, is not only a peril to the union, he is a peril to the larger interests of the nation. He keeps workingmen from their natural organization, deprives them of the strength that union brings, and thwarts all attempts to train men for industrial democracy. Instead of discipline and preparation for the task of the future, instead of deep-grounded experience in coöperative effort, we shall get, if strike-breakers and blind legislators and brutal policemen and prejudiced judges and visionless employers prevail, despair and hate and servile rebellions.

There are certain preliminaries of civilization which the great mass of workingmen have not yet won. They have not yet won a living wage, they have not yet won anything like security of employment, they have not yet won respect from the government, they have not yet won the right to be consulted as to the conditions under which they work. Until they do, it is idle to talk about industrial peace, and folly to look for "reasonable" adjustments of difficulties. Reason begins when men have enough power to command respect; a coöperative solution of industrial problems is possible only when all the partners to the coöperation must listen to each other. Until labor is powerful enough to compel that, it cannot trust to the benevolence of its masters,—it has to be suspicious, it has to cling to the few weapons left it, for labor is right in supposing that no national conscience and no employers' conscience yet exhibited are adequate.

There are certain occupations where workingmen have won these preliminaries of civilized life. The most notable example is in railroading, where the Brotherhoods have become a real part of the industrial structure. They are so powerful that they can't be left out. More than that, they are so powerful that they don't have to flirt with insurrection. It is the weak unions, the unorganized and shifting workers, who talk sabotage and flare up into a hundred little popgun rebellions. Guerilla warfare is the only tactic open to weakness. But where unions can meet the employers on a real equality, as railroad workers can, there you will find very little insurrectionary talk.

You will meet in these powerful unions what radical labor leaders call conservatism. That is a very interesting accusation. The rail-

road men have won wages and respect far beyond anything that the
I.W.W. can hope for. They have power which makes the I.W.W.
look insignificant. If the I.W.W. could win for the unskilled anything like the position and responsibility that railroad men enjoy,
it would have achieved something that might well be called a social
revolution. The fact is that the railroad men are "conservatives"
in the labor world, just as the Swiss are conservatives among the
nations. They have won the very things the lack of which makes rebellion necessary. For if men are ground down in poverty, if the
rights of assemblage and free speech are denied them, if their pro-
tests are ineffective and despised, then rebellion is the only possible
way out. But when there is something like a democracy where wrong
is not a matter of life and death, but of better and worse, then the
preliminaries of civilization have been achieved, and more deliberate
tactics become possible.

The I.W.W., the anarchists and the syndicalists know this. That
is why the reformer is an object of special hatred amongst them.
They say, quite rightly, that reform undermines the revolutionary
spirit, and substitutes for flaming impatience and heroic moods, concrete adjustments and grudging change. They say that only passionate revolt can redeem society from stagnant mediocrity. They
prefer the atmosphere of temporary rebellion to the somewhat slow-
footed and generally uninspired method of a clumsy democracy.
Thus the I.W.W. makes no real effort to build up permanent
unions. That is to say, it does not look with favor upon the cohesive
power of funds and fraternal benefits. I have heard Haywood say
that when a union had something to lose, the spontaneity of rebellion was gone.[6] He hopes to unite wage-earners by militant feeling,
rather than to knit them together by common discipline and common interests. The I.W.W. prefers revolt to solidarity—of course,
it imagines that it can have workers united and militant too. But
in practice it is quite ready to destroy union for the sake of mili-
tancy.

Syndicalists and anarchists half recognize the fact that only a
small minority of the workers can be aroused to bitter revolt. So
they have begun to sing the praises of a "conscious minority." In

[6] Lippmann and the I.W.W. leader "Big Bill" Haywood had argued labor tactics
at Mabel Dodge's salon.

other words they have abandoned the path of democracy, because it is incompatible with the temper they most admire. Workers who were really effectively organized would produce great changes in our social structure, but they would have to act with a deliberation that no temperamental anarchist can stomach. This is the paradox of the labor movement, that those who can't overthrow society dream of doing it, while those who could, don't want to. If there is one occupation where syndicalist tactics might work, it would be on the railroads. A small minority could paralyze the country and precipitate a General Strike. But American railroad men are not likely to do this because they don't need to. They have a stake in the country, a genuine representation in public opinion, and they can at all times secure a respectful hearing. If that were taken away from them, if their unions were disintegrated, they too might take to conspiracy.

It is a commonplace of radicalism that power makes for peace. It is deeply true of the labor movement that the alternatives before it are powerful peace and weak insurrection. Thus if the I.W.W. should succeed in organizing the unskilled on any extensive scale, the I.W.W., as we know it, would have abolished itself. For the unions which were created would inevitably seek a different type of leader: men of administrative capacity who can wield power without exhausting it. The extreme weakness of the unskilled workers has made them listen so eagerly to the large hopes of men like Haywood, Ettor and Giovannitti.[7] Wherever democracy is feeble vague insurrection is its dream. And so the civilized hope for labor is conditioned upon its conquest of power in the life of the nation. This alone will make peaceful adjustments possible, not the moral guardianship of the employers, not the charity of the community. It is the rich who don't need ready cash, it is the strong who don't have to fight.

I know how offensive all this will be to refined and sensitive people. Those who believe in disarmament have come to think that the possession of power is a temptation to use it. Perhaps that is true. But wage-earners have no choice in the matter. If they abandon power, employers will not abandon theirs. To preach

[7] The I.W.W. leaders Joseph Ettor and Arturo Giovannitti had played prominent roles in the Lawrence strike.

mere peace, then, is to preach a docile exploitation. Perhaps when society has learned to respect labor, then society and labor will disarm. But that day is not our day. It is not pleasant, but it's true: if labor turns the other cheek, that cheek will be smitten without much compunction. For the Golden Rule works best among equals.

So the real peril to the nation from the side of labor is the existence of great masses of unorganized, and perhaps unorganizable, workers. From them will come most of the street-fights, the beatings and the sabotage. They have no share in the country, they have "nothing to lose but their chains." But with the tactics open to them they haven't "a world to win." They can parade and shout, call the police "cossacks," and talk revolution. But they have to put up with the pettiest gains.

To the weakness of all labor is to be ascribed its lack of interest in the efficiency of industry. An employer will tell you in one breath that he will stand no interference with "his" business, and in the next that his employees take no interest in that business. Of course they don't. They haven't any *interest*. They are unconsulted outsiders. You might as well expect an Indian peasant to be interested in the administrative efficiency of the British government. What possibility is there for a sense of craftsmanship when you are a mere hired hand? What incentive have wage-earners to take a personal interest in the problems of industry, when nobody asks their advice, and everybody resents it? If labor is apathetic, hostile to efficiency, without much pride, it is because labor is not a part of industrial management. People don't take a sympathetic interest in the affairs of state until they are voting members of the state. You can't expect civic virtue from a disfranchised class, nor industrial virtue from the industrially disfranchised.

The labor problem, then, is at bottom the effort of wage-earners to achieve power. And that effort points, neither to insurrection nor inefficiency, but to a correction of the weakness and unimportance which make rebellion necessary and destroy an interest in work. This is what the fighting and turmoil are about. Employers will tell you that they don't mind raising wages half so much as they mind giving unions "something to say." Yet "something to say" is just what the workers want. They know that better conditions are very elusive unless they have the power to enforce them, to see that what is given with one hand is not taken away with the other. The great battles of labor are for recognition of the union or to maintain its integrity. It happens that the great battles of American history have also been fought for independence and union.

When these prime conditions are achieved, labor's demands tend toward an increasing share of control. The right of summary discharge is the issue in many a strike. For unions will encroach more and more on matters of discipline: they are seeking to raise themselves to a partnership in the management. It is no idle guess to suppose that they will come to demand the right to choose their own foremen, perhaps to elect some of the directors, and to take not only wages, but a percentage of the profits.

It is obvious, of course, that this assumption of power cannot go to indefinite limits. There are people concerned about industry besides the workers in it. The consumers will have a control, and the state, which while it includes workers and purchasers is larger than particular groups of them, the state too will have a say about the control of industry. It is one of the immense problems of the future to adjust these conflicts and to reach some working plan. But that problem has only outlined itself dimly as yet. Labor is far from having achieved anything like its legitimate influence in the conduct of industry, and the best hope for future adjustment lies in the immense discipline that power will enforce upon the worker.

In this movement to eat into economic absolutism, very perplexing questions, of course, arise. What is the proper structure for a union? Shall it be organized by crafts, or occupations, or industries? With amalgamation or by federation? How shall the unions be governed: by representatives or by direct vote? In fact, there is hardly a problem of constitutional government which doesn't appear in acute form among the workers. And in passing, one might suggest that scholars who wish to see sovereignty in the making cannot do better than to go among the unions. They will find the initiative and referendum in constant use. They will find all phases of corruption and misrepresentation: the disappointments of indiscriminate democracy and the blight of officialism. There is a long history of bickerings over sectional interests as against national ones, home rule, devolution,—for all of these matters are, under different phrases, of course, the daily subject of union discussion.

The solutions are of very great interest to the nation. For on the capacity of labor to develop an efficient government for itself hangs the decision as to how much responsibility the unions can afford to assume. It is the development of a citizenship in industry that the labor movement has before it. It will have to work out the intricate problem of popular control in relation to technical administration. Any useful kind of industrial training, then, has got to serve this need. It is obvious that mere skill at some one process is no preparation. Nor is a generalized knowledge of industry enough. There must be added to it an understanding of what may be called the political problem of labor, the questions that arise in its efforts at self-government, in its adjustments to the world that surrounds the industry.

There is nothing simple and perfectly reassuring ahead. With wage-earners about one-tenth organized, unionism has a gigantic problem before it. And there seems to be no limit to the methods by which organization is thwarted. Race is played against race, religion against religion, there are spies, black-lists, lockouts, thugs, evictions, the denial of free speech and the right to assemble. Things are done in America today which are more lurid than melodrama. After thinking of the promise of the labor movement, you have to turn back to present realities, to that brutal struggle in West Virginia, for example, where a gatling gun mounted on a railroad car was run through a mining village at night, "spitting bullets at the rate of two hundred and fifty a minute."

You think of the powerful organizations ready to combat every sign of unionism, of the congestion of immigrants in the labor market, of the hostility of courts and newspapers to the preliminaries of industrial democracy. I don't know, no one knows, whether labor can realize its promise. The odds seem to be overwhelming. There is a real struggle, a trial of strength. It is not yet a matter of justice in which "there is much to be said on both sides." Labor is still fighting to be admitted to the sphere of human society where it is possible to talk of adjusting difficulties. A few workers, like the skilled railroad men, have just about climbed in. But the great mass has not been made part of that world where decisions are made and policies formulated. The unions are struggling to give the wage-earners representation, and that is why the hopes of democracy are bound up with the labor movement. Bound up, not with its words and dogmas, but with the purpose which animates it. Labor needs criticism, needs inventive thought, needs advice and help. But no one can give any of these things who has not grasped with full sympathy that impulse for industrial democracy which is the key to the movement. Without this sympathy the crudity of labor is shocking, the intrigue of labor politics disgusting, the tone of labor discouraging; but with an understanding that a new interest is rising to power it is possible, I think, to find a glimmer of meaning in the bewildering intricacy of the whole matter.

6

The Funds of Progress

By this time, I imagine, the reader will be wondering how these modern ambitions are to be financed. For at the core of all the spiritual demands of the labor movement there is a perfectly frank desire for more wealth. The consumer attempting to pull down prices and jack up quality is making the same demand from another angle. And all through society there runs an increasing agitation for better cities, for a more attractive countryside, for enlarged schools, for health campaigns, for a thousand elements of civilization which cost money and pay in happiness. Where is this money to come from? It must come, says the radical, out of unearned wealth.

But what is unearned wealth? Rent of land, says the single taxer; the tariff tax, says the free trader; watered stock, inherited fortunes, speculative profits, monopoly prices,—these have been named; rent, interest, and dividends, say the socialists. Most employers would point to the wages of inefficient workingmen.

There is one item of agreement: a fund of wealth exists which to-day is being diverted into the pockets of those who do no adequate service—we may call that fund the Social Surplus. It is made up of all the leaks, the useless payments, the idle demands, the inefficiency, the extortion and parasitism of industrial life. This surplus is the legitimate fund of progress.

It is quite clear that no sane man wishes to attack the economic life of a nation in any way that would make it less productive. So when editorial writers and financial experts cry out that a certain tax will ruin industry, they are making a charge which would be convincing if it were true. But the trouble is that nine times out of ten they are either dishonest or superstitious. They complain on every occasion with the slightest provocation. They have cried "wolf" so often that reformers don't listen any more. Business has a way of shouting before it is hurt, and pretending that the least little thing is the sack of the world. Every labor law, every business regulation, every insignificant tariff change calls forth clouds of gloom pierced by a shriek that panic is upon us. It is a pity, for the chief effect of this latent hysteria is to neutralize whatever wisdom business men have to give. Now in the years to come, we shall have to cut into the unearned surplus of industry. If it is done wisely, the attack will be confined to what is really unearned. But the opinions of business men may be no index of the truth. They will, I fear, make just as much commotion over a tax that hits the surplus as over one that hits production itself. When we attack the parasite they will say it is the tree.

Yet the modern business man is actually beginning to locate portions of the surplus. The worker who loafs is the first to catch his eye; then the inefficient worker. So business men are advocating industrial education as a way of making labor more productive. To employ a less productive worker when a more efficient one is available would be just so much waste. In large business there is a constant effort to cut down costs, and one of the vaunted achievements of the trusts has been to eliminate a host of middlemen, drawing profits for work that need not be done under a proper organization. Then too, a big item in many business houses is rent paid to a landlord. The more progressive manufacturers are beginning to wonder whether the cost of government couldn't be shifted on to these landlords, who seem to be a very unproductive class. So the single tax makes headway among business men, under the slogan "Untax industry."

This effort to organize out of existence the unproductive is what is meant by an attack on "unearned" wealth. Wherever you can substitute a machine for a man, a good worker for a poor one, a few salaried managers for an army of jobbers, you have located some of the social surplus. The trusts have been the leaders in this work. They have given us a definition of unearned income. It is a payment for an unnecessary service.

Take the case against the landlord. There are people who say that no individual has a right to own any portion of the globe. The earth belongs to all the people born on to it. But that is one of those unimpeachable sentiments which mean very little in practice. In the early days on this continent it would probably have been impossible to open up the West unless land was given away to the settler. There is no sense then in describing the economic rent some of those settlers took as unearned wealth. The case against the landlord is made out only when society has some better way of administering its natural resources. If New York City were capable of managing its land, then landlordism in New York City would have become unnecessary and parasitic. But if the city isn't capable of that task, if it can, on the other hand, spend wisely twenty per cent. of the ground values, then landlordism has become twenty per cent. parasitic.

Take the charge of the socialist that not only rent of land but interest on capital is unearned. Most socialists seem to imagine that interest is in its very nature a useless payment. The idea is clearly too simple for the facts. Interest would be unearned if society had devised some means of creating capital that didn't require saving by individuals. To a certain extent society has done that. For example, when a city starts to build a subway it needs capital. It can go to the bankers, but it will have to pay a very high rate of interest. It may be that the city could do its own banking and secure the money at a lower rate of interest. In that case the difference between the lower and the higher rate would represent unearned wealth. Now the time may come, I am inclined to think it is sure to come, when the government will be operating the basic industries, railroads, mines, and so forth. It will be possible then to finance government enterprise out of the profits of its industries, to eliminate interest, and substitute collective saving.

There is no blanket case against the landlord or the capitalists. The socialist contention stands or falls by men's ability to propose industrial methods which operate without the need of paying rent or interest. The landlord is an old-fashioned instrument to be superseded as fast as a less costly one can be devised. He is like the stage-coach, useless only when the railroad is possible. He is like the jobber, useless when he is no longer needed. He is like the telegraph, too costly when the wireless is possible. He is like the $100,000 man on a salary, unnecessary when better and less expensive men are ready to do the work.

This it seems to me is the way we shall locate the funds of progress. When a reform administration comes into power it generally begins by cutting out the sinecures, consolidating jobs, substituting competent for incompetent officials. The money saved can be devoted to social purposes. Well, a very capable administration does not stop there. It may eliminate the contractor, and do government work directly, and save a great deal of money in the process. If it has wider plans, it may look for new sources of wealth, as Lloyd George did in England, it may begin to tap the rent of land. Governments can eat more and more into unearned wealth by income taxes, graded drastically, by inheritance taxes on large fortunes. If these funds are spent for civilization they will not impair industry, they will on the contrary increase its efficiency. The state may encroach continuously. The question at issue always is whether the state can spend the money more wisely than the private individual. Could the government make better use of Mr. Carnegie's huge fortune than Mr. Carnegie does?—that is the problem. Are there better uses to which it might be put than those which Mr. Carnegie has in mind? If there are, then the government is entirely justified in substituting itself for Mr. Carnegie as a dispenser of libraries and peace palaces.

The more competent government becomes, the wider its outlook and the surer its method, the more surplus it will find available. The community is engaged in a competition with rich men as to which can make the better use of the nation's wealth. There is no question of inalienable rights. It is a question of good use and bad use, wise use and foolish use. When Mr. Rockefeller founded the Rockefeller Institute he did something which is wiser than most of what our government has yet shown itself capable. But when millionaires invest in ropes of pearls and flotillas of yachts they tempt the taxing power of even the most stupid government.

The cry is sure to go up that all this is a proposal to destroy "incentive." A debater might reply quickly that there are no end of "incentives" in the world to-day which ought by all means to be destroyed. But the cry would not recur so regularly were there not a genuine fear behind it. Men look at the industrial world to-day, and find that it produces enormous quantities of goods. They reason that any change would result in the production of less goods. That is the logic of their fear.

Perhaps you think I'm unjust, that worldly men could not possibly reason in so muddled a way. Well, leave the editorial writers and the speech-making bankers. Go to the orthodox economists who talk about incentive all the time. Prof. Marshall,[1] for example, refers in one place to "that measurement of motive which is the chief task of economic science." Obviously, if economics could perform such a task it would be one of the most useful sciences in the world. The art of life would have found a very solid basis if we could follow Marshall and measure "the payment that is required to supply a sufficient incentive." But at no point in the whole field of political economy is the withering effect of a bad method so evident as it is in the very pages from which I am quoting. Marshall lays great stress on the measurement of motive. He says that economics leads all the other social sciences, because it deals not only with the *quality* of human motive but with *quantity, measurable in money.*

What ails that idea is that it conceals a vicious circle. Measure motive in terms of money? If a man to-day receives a hundred dollars for a piece of work, the measure of his motive is a hundred dollars. Is it? That is just what remains to be proved. If you take the money paid men to-day as a measure of motive, you assume what you started to discover. For you set out to find what you need to pay him in order to provide an incentive. You end by calling what you did pay him a measure of motive. You have begged the question completely. It is as pure a piece of sophistry as the statement that opium puts you to sleep because it is an opiate.

Supposing you set out to discover how much food a man needs in order to live. You meet a glutton and inquire about his diet. You then announce that what this glutton eats is what this glutton needs. Would you call that science? You meet an anemic person,

[1] The British economist, Alfred Marshall.

register his diet, and announce that the food he consumes is a measure of his needs. This is literally what the orthodox economist does. He meets an economic glutton, a millionaire, and discovers that this man built a railroad, opened up new territory, and took fifty million dollars for the job. That means, says the economist, that in order to provide sufficient incentive for this magnificent enterprise fifty million dollars is required. He meets a half-starved mill-worker, who produces cloth at the rate of nine dollars a week. That proves, says the economist, that you must pay nine dollars a week for this work; to pay any more would be contrary to the principles of economics.

To say that economists measure motive in money is to say in roundabout fashion that whatever is, is necessary; then, adding insult to incompetence, to infer that whatever is, is right. Surely it is obvious as sunlight that people's incomes to-day have only a very slight relation to the "payment that is required to supply a sufficient incentive." In the case of a boy who inherits eighty million dollars from a father who inherited it from the grandfather, it is clear that this income has nothing to do with incentive. Well, all through our social system these crazy anomalies occur. Unskilled labor is bought in the open market for a shabby keep and no provision for wear and tear. Competitive wages are no index of motives: they measure what a man has to take in order to live. Skilled labor does a bit better by organizing a monopoly, and fighting for higher pay. The real directors of industry are paid fixed salaries for their ability, and make fortunes "on the side." Inventive genius lives from hand to mouth, and some smart person capitalizes its achievements. It pays better to own land than to cultivate it, to draw dividends than to create them. The great fortunes go to those who control the franchises, the forests, the water-powers, the mines, not to the engineers, the administrators, and the workers who are hired to use them. If I can "corner" the wheat supply, if I can make food scarce, if I can contrive some new fraud or stimulate some new madness in fashions, I can grow rich beyond the dreams of honest labor. Money measures incentive: there is no real relation to-day between money-making and useful work.

Power, position, pull, custom, weakness, oversupply, the class monopoly of higher education, inheritance, accident, the strategy of industrial war—these are the things which determine income—not the incentive which is necessary. The work of the world is not done because the producers get what stimulates them to their best effort. It is done under the compulsion of circumstances, grounded in habit, and the lure of big rewards is in the rarest cases a lure to human service. That is why the industrial world is capable of tremendous reorganization without impairing its efficiency. A better distribution of incomes would increase that efficiency by diverting a great fund of wealth from the useless to the useful members of society. To cut off the income of the useless will not impair their efficiency. They have none to impair. It will, in fact, compel them to acquire a useful function.

Now the working class has very excellent uses for money that it can secure. It invests it directly in human life, in the food, clothing, shelter, and recreation which are its basis. So the pressure of the labor movement is a force that can make for a wiser use of wealth. If employers find that they "cannot" pay higher wages, their real business is not to resist labor, but to increase the efficiency of production so that they can. They will have to learn to finance industry better, they will have to eliminate the sinecures of their cousins and their uncles, they will have to scale down capitalization, and do without the hundred and one middlemen who extract a profit.

That is the only way they can meet the pressure of labor from one side and of the consumer on the other. Both of those movements are really demands for a wiser management of business. Both of them are interested in industrial efficiency. This may seem a strange thing to say in the face of labor's hostility to labor-saving devices. But the reason for the hostility is that labor at present gains very little, almost nothing, by its increased productivity. When labor and the consumer really share in industrial progress, as they will when they are powerful enough, we shall have two forces constantly at work to eliminate the parasite and abolish waste.

The commercial adventurer has no real interest in efficiency. Between useful service and some mad freak the decisive point is which will pay him the most. But consumers and workingmen are interested directly in making industry produce the greatest quantity and the best quality of goods at the least possible cost in effort. They are made poorer by money devoted to producing useless luxuries. They pay all the cost of waste, parasitism, and inefficiency. That is why the real progress of industry is bound up intimately with their demands.

The more they press the better. I know how much this will harass the business man. But his necessity will be the mother of invention. When he finds that he faces on one side an organized labor movement, on another the organized consumer, and on another the taxing power of the state, when he is no longer able to cover waste by reducing wages or raising prices, then he will have to devote himself more and more to the real business of industrial management. He will begin to cut down his extravagant selling costs, he will have to finance his enterprise less expensively, he will have to squeeze out watered stock, he will have to scale down futile salaries, do without some of his "side" ventures, spend less time on the stock market, and give the best of his thought to coördinating the industry.

These necessities will be the opportunity of the business man with a scientific training. Already we are beginning to see that in the light of its possibilities, industry to-day is inconceivably wasteful. The raw product is won from the earth, it is transported hundreds of miles over expensive railroads, it passes through ten or twenty different manipulators, is manufactured, and passes again through an infinitely complicated series of operations to the ultimate consumer. The great water-power resources of this country are said to be not one-seventh developed. Yet their primary power alone "exceeds our entire mechanical power in use, would operate every mill, drive every spindle, propel every train and boat, and light every city, town, and village in the country." [2] Coal burned on the American locomotive is estimated by the Railway Age Gazette to be only 45% efficient. The whole conservation movement in its infinite ramifications is an answer to the pressing demands that people are making upon industry. So far in America we have been spendthrifts with our resources, letting coal lie half

[2] J. Russell Smith, *Industrial and Commercial Geography* (New York: Henry Holt and Company, 1913), p. 398.

mined, skinning the forests, and obtaining by agriculture a yield that shames us in the eyes of the European farmer. The wealth exists to pay for democracy. Our dreams are not idle. We are not a poor people who need fill our minds with gorgeous and impossible visions. Labor can go ahead with its demands, the consumer with his, we can enter upon social works to transform our sooty life into something more worthy of our dignity. There are huge wastes to be eliminated, parasitic incomes to be cut off, large classes of people to be turned from useless into useful effort, great inventions to be utilized. But these things will be done only if there is constant pressure on the industrial system from those who work in it and live by it.

7

"A Nation of Villagers"

—*Bernard Shaw*

It has been said that no trust could have been created without breaking the law. Neither could astronomy in the time of Galileo. If you build up foolish laws and insist that invention is a crime, well—then it is a crime. That is undeniably true, but not very interesting. Of course, you can't possibly treat the trusts as crimes. First of all, nobody knows what the trust laws mean. The spectacle of an enlightened people trying in vain for twenty-five years to find out the intention of a statute that it has enacted—that is one of those episodes that only madmen can appreciate. You see, it is possible to sympathize with the difficulties of a scholar trying to decipher the hieroglyphics of some ancient people, but when statesmen can't read the things they've written themselves, it begins to look as if some imp had been playing pranks. The men who rule this country to-day were all alive, and presumably sane, when the Sherman Act was passed. They all say in public that it is a great piece of legislation—an "exquisite instrument" someone called it the other day. The highest paid legal intelligence has concentrated on the Act. The Supreme Court has interpreted it many times, ending with the enormous assumption that reason had something to do with the law.[1] The Supreme Court was denounced for this: the reformers said that if there was any

[1] In *Standard Oil Co. v. United States*, 221 U.S. 1 (1911), Chief Justice Edward D. White enunciated the "rule of reason"; the Sherman Act, he insisted, prohibited only unreasonable restraints of trade.

reason in the law, the devil himself had got hold of it. As I write, Congress is engaged in trying to define what it thinks it means by the Act. . . .[2]
That uncertainty hasn't prevented a mass of indictments, injunctions, lawsuits. It has, if anything, invited them. But of course, you can't enforce the criminal law against every "unfair" business practice. Just try to imagine the standing army of inspectors, detectives, prosecutors, and judges, the city of courthouses and jails, the enormous costs, and the unremitting zeal—if you cannot see the folly, at least see the impossibility of the method. To work with it seriously would not only bring business to a standstill, it would drain the energy of America more thoroughly than the bitterest foreign war. Visualize life in America, if you can, when the government at Washington and forty-eight state governments really undertook not our present desultory pecking, but a systematic enforcement of the criminal law. The newspapers would enjoy it for a week, and everybody would be excited; in two weeks it would be a bore; in six, there would be such a revolt that everyone, radical and conservative, would be ready to wreck the government and hang the attorney-general. For these "criminal" practices are so deep in the texture of our lives; they affect so many, their results are so intimate that anything like a "surgical" cutting at evil would come close to killing the patient.

If the anti-trust people really grasped the full meaning of what they said, and if they really had the power or the courage to do what they propose, they would be engaged in one of the most destructive agitations that America has known. They would be breaking up the beginning of a collective organization, thwarting the possibility of coöperation, and insisting upon submitting industry to the wasteful, the planless scramble of little profiteers. They would make impossible any deliberate and constructive use of our natural resources, they would thwart any effort to form the great industries into coordinated services, they would preserve commercialism as the undisputed master of our lives, they would lay a premium on the strategy of industrial war,—they would, if they could. For these anti-trust people have never seen the pos-

[2] Congress's attempt to redefine the anti-trust law resulted in the enactment of the Clayton law on October 15, 1914.

sibilities of organized industries. They have seen only the obvious evils, the birth-pains, the undisciplined strut of youth, the bad manners, the greed, and the trickery. The trusts have been ruthless, of course. No one tried to guide them; they have broken the law in a thousand ways, largely because the law was such that they had to.

At any rate, I should not like to answer before a just tribunal for the harm done this country in the last twenty-five years by the stupid hostility of anti-trust laws. How much they have perverted the constructive genius of this country it is impossible to estimate. They have blocked any policy of welcome and use, they have concentrated a nation's thinking on inessentials, they have driven creative business men to underhand methods, and put a high money value on intrigue and legal cunning, demagoguery and waste. The trusts have survived it all, but in mutilated form, the battered make-shifts of a trampled promise. They have learned every art of evasion—the only art reformers allowed them to learn.

It is said that the economy of trusts is unreal. Yet no one has ever tried the economies of the trust in any open, deliberate fashion. The amount of energy that has had to go into repelling stupid attack, the adjustments that had to be made underground— it is a wonder the trusts achieved what they did to bring order out of chaos, and forge an instrument for a nation's business. You have no more right to judge the trusts by what they are than to judge the labor movement by what it is. Both of them are in that preliminary state where they are fighting for existence, and any real outburst of constructive effort has been impossible for them.

But revolutions are not stopped by blind resistance. They are only perverted. And as an exhibition of blind resistance to a great promise, the trust campaign of the American democracy is surely unequalled. Think of contriving correctives for a revolution, such as ordering business men to compete with each other. It is as if we said: 'Let not thy right hand know what thy left hand doeth; let thy right hand fight thy left hand, and in the name of God let neither win." Bernard Shaw remarked several years ago that "after all, America is not submitting to the Trusts without a struggle. The first steps have already been taken by the village constable. He is no doubt preparing a new question for immigrants"

. . . after asking them whether they are anarchists or polygamists, he is to add " 'Do you approve of Trusts?' but pending this supreme measure of national defense he has declared in several states that trusts will certainly be put in the stocks and whipped." There has been no American policy on the trust question: there has been merely a widespread resentment. The small local competitors who were wiped out became little centers of bad feeling: these nationally organized industries were looked upon as foreign invaders. They were arrogant, as the English in Ireland or the Germans in Alsace, and much of the feeling for local democracy attached itself to the revolt against these national despotisms. The trusts made enemies right and left: they squeezed the profits of the farmer, they made life difficult for the shopkeeper, they abolished jobbers and travelling salesmen, they closed down factories, they exercised an enormous control over credit through their size and through their eastern connections. Labor was no match for them, state legislatures were impotent before them. They came into the life of the simple American community as a tremendous revolutionary force, upsetting custom, changing men's status, demanding a readjustment for which people were unready. Of course, there was anti-trust feeling; of course, there was a blind desire to smash them. Men had been ruined and they were too angry to think, too hard pressed to care much about the larger life which the trusts suggested.

This feeling came to a head in Bryan's famous "cross of gold" speech in 1896. "When you come before us and tell us that we shall disturb your business interests, we reply that you have disturbed our business interests by your action. . . . The man who is employed for wages is as much a business man as his employers. The attorney in a country town is as much a business man as the corporation counsel in a great metropolis. The merchant at the crossroads store is as much a business man as the merchant of New York. The farmer . . . is as much a business man as the man who goes upon the Board of Trade and bets upon the price of grain. The miners . . . It is for these that we speak . . . we are fighting in the defense of our homes, our families, and posterity." What Bryan was really defending was the old and simple life of America, a life that was doomed by the great organization that had come into the world. He thought he was fighting the plutocracy: as a matter of fact he was fighting something much deeper than that; he was fighting the larger scale of human life. The Eastern money power controlled the new industrial system, and Bryan fought it. But what he and his people hated from the bottom of their souls were the economic conditions which had upset the old life of the prairies, made new demands upon democracy, introduced specialization and science, had destroyed village loyalties, frustrated private ambitions, and created the impersonal relationships of the modern world.

Bryan has never been able to adjust himself to the new world in which he lives. That is why he is so irresistibly funny to sophisticated newspaper men. His virtues, his habits, his ideas, are the simple, direct, shrewd qualities of early America. He is the true Don Quixote of our politics, for he moves in a world that has ceased to exist.

He is a more genuine conservative than some propertied bigot. Bryan stands for the popular tradition of America, whereas most of his enemies stand merely for the power that is destroying that tradition. Bryan is what America was; his critics are generally defenders of what America has become. And neither seems to have any vision of what America is to be. Yet there has always been great power behind Bryan, the power of those who in one way or another were hurt by the greater organization that America was developing. The Populists were part of that power. La Follette and the insurgent Republicans expressed it. It was easily a political majority of the American people. The Republican Party disintegrated under the pressure of the revolt. The Bull Moose gathered much of its strength from it. The Socialists have got some of it. But in 1912 it swept the Democratic Party, and by a combination of circumstances, carried the country. The plutocracy was beaten in politics, and the power that Bryan spoke for in 1896, the forces that had made muckraking popular, captured the government. They were led by a man who was no part of the power that he represented.

Woodrow Wilson is an outsider capable of skilled interpretation. He is an historian, and that has helped him to know the older tradition of America. He is a student of theory, and like most theorists of his generation he is deeply attached to the doctrines that swayed the world when America was founded.

But Woodrow Wilson at least knows that there is a new world. "There is one great basic fact which underlies all the questions that are discussed on the political platform at the present moment. That singular fact is that nothing is done in this country as it was done twenty years ago. We are in the presence of a new organization of society. . . . We have changed our economic conditions, absolutely, from top to bottom; and, with our economic society, the organization of our life." You could not make a more sweeping statement of the case. The President is perfectly aware of what has happened, and he says at the very outset that "our laws still deal with us on the basis of the old system . . . the old positive formulas do not fit the present problems."

You wait eagerly for some new formula. The new formula is this: "I believe the time has come when the governments of this country, both state and national, have to set the stage, and set it very minutely and carefully, for the doing of justice to men in every relationship of life." Now that is a new formula, because it means a willingness to use the power of government much more extensively.

But for what purpose is this power to be used? There, of course, is the rub. It is to be used to *restore* our politics to their full spiritual vigor *again,* and our national life, whether in trade, in industry, or in what concerns us only as families and individuals, to its purity, its self-respect, and its *pristine* strength and freedom." The ideal is the old ideal, the ideal of Bryan, the method is the new one of government interference.

That, I believe, is the inner contradiction of Woodrow Wilson. He knows that there is a new world demanding new methods, but he dreams of an older world. He is torn between the two. It is a very deep conflict in him between what he knows and what he feels.

His feeling is, as he says, for "the man on the make." "For my part, I want the pigmy to have a chance to come out" . . . "Just let some of the youngsters I know have a chance and they'll give these gentlemen points. Lend them a little money. They can't get any now. See to it that when they have got a local market they can't be squeezed out of it." Nowhere in his speeches will you find any sense that it may be possible to organize the fundamental industries on some deliberate plan for national service. He is thinking always about somebody's chance to build up a profitable business; he likes the idea that somebody can beat somebody else, and the small business man takes on the virtues of David in a battle with Goliath.

"Have you found trusts that thought as much of their men as they did of their machinery?" he asks, forgetting that few people have ever found competitive textile mills or clothing factories that did. There isn't an evil of commercialism that Wilson isn't ready to lay at the door of the trusts. He becomes quite reckless in his denunciation of the New Devil—Monopoly—and of course, by contrast the competitive business takes on a halo of light. It is amazing how clearly he sees the evils that trusts do, how blind he is to the evils that his supporters do. You would think that the trusts were the first oppressors of labor; you would think they were the first business organization that failed to achieve the highest possible efficiency. The pretty record of competition throughout the Nineteenth Century is forgotten. Suddenly all that is a glorious past which we have lost. You would think that competitive commercialism was really a generous, chivalrous, high-minded stage of human culture.

"We design that the limitations on private enterprise shall be removed, so that the next generation of youngsters, as they come along, will not have to become protégés of benevolent trusts, but will be free to go about making their own lives what they will; so that we shall taste again the full cup, not of charity, but of liberty,—the only wine that ever refreshed and renewed the spirit of a people." That cup of liberty—we may well ask him to go back to Manchester, to Paterson to-day, to the garment trades of New York, and taste it for himself.

The New Freedom means the effort of small business men and farmers to use the government against the larger collective organization of industry. Wilson's power comes from them; his feeling is with them; his thinking is for them. Never a word of understanding for the new type of administrator, the specialist, the professionally trained business man; practically no mention of the consumer—

even the tariff is for the business man; no understanding of the new demands of labor, its solidarity, its aspiration for some control over the management of business; no hint that it may be necessary to organize the fundamental industries of the country on some definite plan so that our resources may be developed by scientific method instead of by men "on the make"; no friendliness for the larger, collective life upon which the world is entering, only a constant return to the commercial chances of young men trying to set up in business. That is the push and force of this New Freedom, a freedom for the little profiteer, but no freedom for the nation from the narrowness, the poor incentives, the limited vision of small competitors,—no freedom from clamorous advertisement, from wasteful selling, from duplication of plants, from unnecessary enterprise, from the chaos, the welter, the strategy of industrial war.

There is no doubt, I think, that President Wilson and his party represent primarily small business in a war against the great interests. Socialists speak of his administration as a revolution within the bounds of capitalism. Wilson doesn't really fight the oppressions of property. He fights the evil done by large property-holders to small ones. The temper of his administration was revealed very clearly when the proposal was made to establish a Federal Trade Commission. It was suggested at once by leading spokesmen of the Democratic Party that corporations with a capital of less than a million dollars should be exempted from supervision. Is that because little corporations exploit labor or the consumer less? Not a bit of it. It is because little corporations are in control of the political situation.

But there are certain obstacles to the working out of the New Freedom. First of all, there was a suspicion in Wilson's mind, even during the campaign, that the tendency to large organization was too powerful to be stopped by legislation. So he left open a way of escape from the literal achievement of what the New Freedom seemed to threaten. *"I am for big business,"* he said, *"and I am against the trusts."* That is a very subtle distinction, so subtle, I suspect, that no human legislation will ever be able to make it. The distinction is this: big business is a business that has survived competition; a trust is an arrangement to do away with competition. But when competition is done away with, who is the Solomon wise enough to know whether the result was accomplished by superior efficiency or by agreement among the competitors or by both?

The big trusts have undoubtedly been built up in part by superior business ability, and by successful competition, but also by ruthless competition, by underground arrangements, by an intricate series of facts which no earthly tribunal will ever be able to disentangle. And why should it try? These great combinations are here. What interests us is not their history but their future. The point is whether you are going to split them up, and if so into how many parts. Once split, are they to be kept from coming together again? Are you determined to prevent men who could coöperate from cooperating? Wilson seems to imply that a big business which has survived competition is to be let alone, and the trusts attacked. But as there is no real way of distinguishing between them, he leaves the question just where he found it: he must choose between the large organization of business and the small.

It's here that his temperament and his prejudices clash with fact and necessity. He really would like to disintegrate large business. "Are you not eager for the time," he asks, "when your sons shall be able to look forward to becoming not employees, but heads of some small, it may be, but hopeful business . . . ?" But to what percentage of the population can he hold out that hope? How many small but hopeful steel mills, coal mines, telegraph systems, oil refineries, copper mines, can this country support? A few hundred at the outside. And for these few hundred sons whose "best energies . . . are inspired by the knowledge that they are their own masters with the paths of the world before them," we are asked to give up the hope of a sane, deliberate organization of national industry brought under democratic control.

I submit that it is an unworthy dream. I submit that the intelligent men of my generation can find a better outlet for their energies than in making themselves masters of little businesses. They have the vast opportunity of introducing order and purpose into the business world, of devising administrative methods by which the great resources of the country can be operated on some thought-out plan. They have the whole new field of industrial statesmanship before them, and those who prefer the egotism of some little business are not the ones whose ambitions we need most to cultivate.

But the disintegration which Wilson promised in the New Freedom is not likely to be carried out. One year of public office has toned down the audacity of the campaign speeches so much that Mr. Dooley says you can play the President's messages on a harp. Instead of a "radical reconstruction" we are engaged in signing a "constitution of peace." These big business men who a few months ago showed not the "least promise of disinterestedness" are to-day inspired by "a spirit of accommodation." The President's own Secretary of Commerce, Mr. Redfield, has said to the National Chamber of Commerce that the number of trusts still operating "is conspicuously small." Was ever wish the father to a pleasanter thought? Was ever greater magic wrought with less effort? Or is it that politicians in office have to pretend that what they can't do has happened anyway?

Wilson is against the trusts for many reasons: the political economy of his generation was based on competition and free trade; the Democratic Party is by tradition opposed to a strong central government, and that opposition applies equally well to strong national business,—it is a party attached to local rights, to village patriotism, to humble but ambitious enterprise; its temper has always been hostile to specialization and expert knowledge, because it admires a very primitive man-to-man democracy. Wilson's thought is inspired by that outlook. It has been tempered somewhat by contact with men who have outgrown the village culture, so that Wilson is less hostile to experts, less oblivious to administrative problems than is Bryan. But at the same time his speeches are marked with contempt for the specialist: they play up quite obviously to the old democratic notion that any man can do almost any job. You have always to except the Negro, of course, about whom the Democrats have a totally different tradition. But among white men, special training and expert knowledge are somewhat under suspicion in Democratic circles.

Hostility to large organization is a natural quality in village life. Wilson is always repeating that the old personal relationships of employer and employee have disappeared. He deplores the impersonal nature of the modern world. Now that is a fact not to be passed over lightly. It does change the nature of our problems enormously. Indeed, it is just this breakdown of the old relationships

86

which constitutes the modern problem. So the earlier chapters of this book were devoted to showing how in response to new organization the psychology of business men had changed; how the very nature of property had been altered; how the consumer has had to develop new instruments for controlling the market, and how labor is compelled to organize its power in order not to be trodden by gigantic economic forces.

Nobody likes the present situation very much. But where dispute arises is over whether we can by legislation return to a simpler and more direct stage of civilization. Bryan really hopes to do that, Wilson does too, but his mind is too critical not to have some doubts, and that is why he is against trusts but not against big business. But there is a growing body of opinion which says that communication is blotting out village culture, and opening up national and international thought. It says that bad as big business is to-day, it has a wide promise within it, and that the real task of our generation is to realize it. It looks to the infusion of scientific method, the careful application of administrative technique, the organization and education of the consumer for control, the discipline of labor for an increasing share of the management. Those of us who hold such a belief are pushed from behind by what we think is an irresistible economic development, and lured by a future which we think is possible.

We don't imagine that the trusts are going to drift naturally into the service of human life. We think they can be made to serve it if the American people compel them. We think that the American people may be able to do that if they can adjust their thinking to a new world situation, if they apply the scientific spirit to daily life, and if they can learn to coöperate on a large scale. Those, to be sure, are staggering *ifs*. The conditions may never be fulfilled entirely. But in so far as they are not fulfilled we shall drift along at the mercy of economic forces that we are unable to master. Those who cling to the village view of life may deflect the drift, may batter the trusts about a bit, but they will never dominate business, never humanize its machinery, and they will continue to be the playthings of industrial change.

At bottom the issue is between those who are willing to enter upon an effort for which there is no precedent, and those who aren't.

In a real sense it is an adventure. We have still to explore the new scale of human life which machinery has thrust upon us. We have still to invent ways of dealing with it. We have still to adapt our abilities to immense tasks. Of course, men shudder and beg to be let off in order to go back to the simpler life for which they were trained. Of course, they hope that competition will automatically produce the social results they desire. Of course, they see all the evils of the trust and none of its promise. They can point to the failure of empires and the success of little cities. They can say that we are obliterating men in the vast organizations we are permitting.

But they are not the only people who realize that man as he is to-day is not big enough to master the modern world. It is this realization which has made men speculate on the development of what they call a "collective mind." They hope that somehow we shall develop an intelligence larger than the individual.

I see no evidence for that. There are no minds but human minds so far as our problems go. It seems to me that this notion of a collective mind over and above men and women is simply a myth created to meet difficulties greater than men and women are as yet capable of handling. It is a *deus ex machina* invented to cover an enormous need,—a hope that something outside ourselves will do our work for us. It would be infinitely easier if such a power existed. But I can't see any ground for relying upon it. We shall have, it seems to me, to develop within men and women themselves the power they need. It is an immense ambition, and each man who approaches it must appear presumptuous. But it is the problem of our generation: to analyze the weakness, to attack the obstacles, to search for some of the possibilities, to realize if we can the kind of effort by which we can face the puzzling world in which we live.

Part Two

8

A Big World and Little Men

Those who take city children out into the country for a day's airing can tell you one story after another about how squirrels and rabbits are classed as cats, cattle as horses, sheep as woolly dogs, how green things are just grass, a tree merely a tree. They will tell you that this is the tragedy of urban civilization,—to rear children who live in a half-noticed, carelessly classified universe, as dumb to them as the stony pavements that serve as their playgrounds.

And yet city children are far from being especially dull-witted. They are simply dull to an environment which really does not concern them. A country boy may go fearlessly among restless animals or find a trail through the woods, but a street-urchin will play baseball in the midst of traffic. Yet we feel a pathetic difference between them, for one is competent amidst enduring things, the other is quick about artificial complications.

The city-dweller never meets as a personal problem the elements that have ordered human life, plants and animals, the tides and the winds, forest and hill. He may work at some abstract part of a complicated manufacture, or spend his time in an office where he deals the day long with papers and telephones, the symbols and shadows of events. He has practically no sense of how he is fed, clothed, or housed, has seen no spinning and weaving, mining or reaping. He has witnessed the milking of one cow with mixed astonishment, has forgotten that steaks come from cattle, and mutton chops from sheep, knows that clover occasionally appears with four leaves and signifies good luck, and spring to him means not sowing time, and the opening of streams, but open cars and straw hats. This uprooted person is the despair of all those who love the flavor of words, for his language has gone stale and abstract in a miserly telegraphic speech. That is why literary men are forever hunting up folk songs and seeking out backward peasants in Galway or Cornwall. Among country people words still taste of actual things: contact with sun and rain and earth and harvest turns the simple prose of the day's work into poetry for the starved imaginations of city-bred people. There has been, to be sure, a brave attempt in recent years to admire slang. But one insuperable difficulty stands in the way: city slang has risen out of the interests that meet the thwarted instincts of a restless population, from the bleachers, the poker table, and the saloon. Slang is often vivid but it is too deeply sundered from the older sources of our happiness. It is not set in the spectacle of earth and sky, as the speech of peasants, and it is for the most part trivial, strained, and raucous. Even the slang of lust is feeble, reflected out of halted fantasy and filtered through commercialism. The obscenity of a smoking-room is little more than the sneaking indulgence of peeping Toms, witty at times because it comes as a relief from the seductive wrappings of a finicky culture. But even lust has become elaborate and second-hand.

For the slow movement of the seasons we have substituted the flicker of fashions. The older world changed, but it repeated itself. Birth and youth and age, summer and winter changed the world and left it unaltered. You could think of eternal ideas, for there was beneath the change some permanence. But in our day change is not an illusion but a fact: we do actually move toward novelty, there is invention, and what has never been is created each day.

We are unsettled to the very roots of our being. There isn't a human relation, whether of parent and child, husband and wife, worker and employer, that doesn't move in a strange situation. We are not used to a complicated civilization, we don't know how to behave when personal contact and eternal authority have disappeared. There are no precedents to guide us, no wisdom that wasn't made for a simpler age. We have changed our environment more quickly than we know how to change ourselves.

And so we are literally an eccentric people, our emotional life is disorganized, our passions are out-of-kilter. Those who call themselves radical float helplessly upon a stream amidst the wreckage of old creeds and abortive new ones, and they are inclined to mistake the motion which carries them for their own will. Those who make no pretensions to much theory are twisted about by fashions, "crazes," at the mercy of milliners and dressmakers, theatrical producers, advertising campaigns and the premeditated gossip of the newspapers.

We live in great cities without knowing our neighbors, the loyalties of place have broken down, and our associations are stretched over large territories, cemented by very little direct contact. But this impersonal quality is intolerable: people don't like to deal with abstractions. And so you find an overwhelming demand upon the press for human interest stories, for personal details opened to the vast public. Gossip is organized; and we do by telegraph what was done in the village store.

Institutions have developed a thousand inconsistencies. Our schools, churches, courts, governments were not built for the kind of civilization they are expected to serve. In former times you could make some effort to teach people what they needed to know. It was done badly, but at least it could be attempted. Men knew the kind of problems their children would have to face. But to-day education means a radically different thing. We have to prepare children to meet the unexpected, for their problems will not be the same as their fathers'. To prepare them for the unexpected means to train them in method instead of filling them with facts and rules. They will have to find their own facts and make their own rules, and if schools can't give them that power then schools no longer educate for the modern world.

The churches face a dilemma which is a matter of life and death to them. They come down to us with a tradition that the great things are permanent, and they meet a population that needs above all to understand the meaning and the direction of change. No wonder their influence has declined, no wonder that men fight against the influence they have. Ministers are as bewildered as the rest of us, perhaps a little more so. For they are expected to stand up every week and interpret human life in a way that will vitalize feeling and conduct. And for this work of interpretation they have the simple rules of a village civilization, the injunctions of a pastoral people. Of course they can't interpret life on Sunday so that the interpretation will mean something on Monday. Even supposing that the average minister understood the scientific spirit, had studied sociology, and knew what are the forces which agitate men, even under those circumstances, interpretation would be an almost impossible task. For the least hampered minds, the most imaginative and experienced men, can only stumble through to partial explanations. To ask the clergy to find adequate meaning in this era is to expect each minister to be an inspired thinker. If the churches really could interpret life they would be unable to make room for the congregations; if men felt that they could draw anything like wisdom from them, they would be besieged by bewildered and inquiring people. Think of the lectures people flock to, the political meetings they throng, the dull books they work their way through. It isn't indifference to the great problems that leaves the churches empty; it is the sheer intellectual failure of the churches to meet a sudden change.

The courts have not been able to adjust themselves either. But while people can ignore the churches, they have to fight the courts. They fight blindly without any clear notion as to what they would like the courts to do. They are irritated and constrained by a legal system that was developed in a different civilization, and they find the courts, as Prof. Roscoe Pound [1] says, "doing nothing and obstructing everything." They find that whenever a legislature makes an effort to fit law to the new facts of life, a court is there to nullify the work. They find the courts masters of our political system, and yet these masters will not really take the initiative. They have enormous power, but they refuse the responsibility that goes with it. The courts are making law all the time, of course. Now if they made law that met the new situations, there would be no revolt against the judiciary. The American voters are not doctrinaires. They don't care in any academic way whether Congress, the President, or the courts, frame legislation. They form their opinions almost entirely by the results. If the President can legislate better

[1] Roscoe Pound, professor of law at Harvard, was a leading authority on jurisprudence.

than Congress, as Roosevelt and Wilson could, the people will support the President no matter how many lawyers shout that the rights of Congress are being usurped. If the courts made law that dealt with modern necessities, the people would, I believe, never question their power. It is the bad sociology of judges and their class prejudices that are destroying the prestige of the bench. That bad sociology and those prejudices are in the main due to the fact that judges have not been trained for the modern world, have never learned how to understand its temper.

And of course, when you come to the political structure of our government you find that it has only the faintest relation to actual conditions. Our political constituencies are to American life what the skeleton of a two-humped camel would be to an elephant. One is not made to fit the other's necessities. Take the City of New York for example. For all practical purposes the metropolitan district extends up into Connecticut and across into New Jersey. By "practical purposes" I mean that as a health problem, a transportation problem, a housing problem, a food problem, a police problem, the city which sprawls across three states ought to be treated as one unit. Or take New England: for any decent solution of its transportation difficulties or for any scientific use of its natural resources its state lines are a nuisance. On the other hand, it mustn't be imagined that the old political units are always too small. Far from it: thus many of the vital functions of New York City are managed by the State legislature. The political system which comes down to us from a totally different civilization is sometimes too large in its unit— sometimes too small, but in a thousand bewildering ways its does not fit. Every statesman is hampered by conflicts of jurisdiction, by divided responsibility, by the fact that when he tries to use the government for some public purpose, the government is a clumsy instrument.

The regulation of the trusts is made immensely difficult by the fact that the states are too small, and the nation is often too large. There are natural sections of the country, like the Pacific Coast, the Ohio, the Mississippi valley, and New England which ought for many purposes to act as a unit. No sane person, I suppose, wishes to centralize at Washington all the power that is needed to control business, and yet everyone knows that if you leave that control to the states, there will be no control.

But the fitting of government to the facts of the modern world is sure to be a very difficult task. In the past governments have been organized as territorial units, but with the development of transportation the importance of geography has declined. Men are bound together to-day by common interests far more than by living in the same place. It is the union, the trade association, the grange, the club and the party that command allegiance rather than the county or the state. To anyone who is not fooled by charters and forms, it is evident that functions of government are being developed in these groups which are not mentioned in theoretical discussions of government. Labor unions legislate, Boards of Trade legislate, coöperative societies are governments in a very real sense. They make rules under which people live, often much more compelling ones than those of some official legislature. Now in the Eighteenth Century there was a strong sentiment against any minor sovereignty within the political state. In France, for example, by a law of 1791 all associations were forbidden. Our common law looked upon them with extreme disfavor, and the Sherman Act is an expression of that same feeling. Theorists like ex-President Eliot in our own day are against unions because they establish little governments within the state. But the facts are against the ideas of the Eighteenth Century. The world is so complex that no official government can be devised to deal with it, and men have had to organize associations of all kinds in order to create some order in the world. They will develop more of them, I believe, for these voluntary groupings based on common interests are the only way yet proposed by which a complicated society can be governed. But of course, unofficial sovereignties within the nation create very perplexing problems. They all tend to be imperious, to reach out and absorb more and more. And the attempt to adjust them to each other is a task for which political science is not prepared.

I have merely touched on some of the difficulties which arise in our domestic affairs because the anatomy of our politics does not correspond to the anatomy of our life. When you come to international affairs confusion is compounded. As I write, we are in the midst of the Mexican problem.[2] No one knows how much authority anyone has in that country. There are all sorts of conflicting interests and all sorts of conflicting governments.

Does the fact that Englishmen invest in Mexico entitle the British Empire to some authority in Mexican affairs? Are we the guardians of Mexico, and if so where does our authority end? The new imperialism is no simple affair: it has innumerable gradations of power. As Prof. Beard [3] says: "This newer imperialism does not rest primarily upon the desire for more territory, but rather upon the necessity for markets in which to sell manufactured goods and for opportunities to invest surplus accumulations of capital. It begins in a search for trade, advances to intervention on behalf of the interests involved, thence to protectorates, and finally to annexation." Diplomacy now talks about "effective occupation," "hinterland," "sphere of influence" and "Sphere of Legitimate Aspiration." [4]

One of the curious ironies of history is that after many generations of effort to establish popular government in a few countries, the real interests of the world have overflowed frontiers and eluded democracy. We are just about to establish a democratic state, and we find that capitalism has become international. It seems as if we were always a little too late for the facts. We are now engaged in building up for the world a few of the primitive devices of internal affairs. A code of law, a few half-hearted, impotent courts, treaties, and a little international policing. But all these things, many of which express the fondest hopes of sensible men, are very little more than arrangements between antagonistic nations. Anything like a world-wide coöperative democracy is as yet no part of the expectation of any unsentimental person.

[2] In February 1913, the idealistic visionary, Francisco I. Madero, who had led the Mexican revolution of 1911, was deposed and murdered by General Victoriano Huerta. Wilson refused to recognize Huerta and sought to aid the Constitutionalists led by Venustiano Carranza. Wilson's well-intentioned efforts ended disastrously, for Carranza and his followers were as strongly opposed as Huerta to American intervention in Mexican affairs. In April 1914, Wilson antagonized all elements in Mexico when he ordered the U.S. Navy to occupy Vera Cruz. Wilson's desire for peace led to bloodshed, and his desire to secure constitutional government for Mexico resulted in almost universal hostility to the United States south of the border.

[3] The American historian and political scientist, Charles A. Beard.

[4] Graham Wallas, *Human Nature in Politics* (Boston: Houghton Mifflin Co., 1909), p. 161.

Now anyone who has talked as much about the industrial problem as I have in these chapters is, of course, expected to present a "solution." But as a matter of fact there can be no such thing as a "solution" in the sense which most people understand the word. When you solve a puzzle, you're done with it, but the industrial puzzle has no single key. Nor is there such a thing for it as a remedy or a cure. You have in a very literal sense to *educate* the industrial situation, to draw out its promise, discipline and strengthen it.

It means that you have to do a great variety of things to industry, invent new ones to do, and keep on doing them. You have to make a survey of the natural resources of the country. On the basis of that survey you must draw up a national plan for their development. You must eliminate waste in mining, you must conserve the forests so that their fertility is not impaired, so that stream flow is regulated, and the waterpower of the country made available. You must bring to the farmer a knowledge of scientific agriculture, help him to organize coöperatively, use the taxing power to prevent land speculation and force land to the best use, coördinate markets, build up rural credits, and create in the country a life that shall really be interesting.

You have the intricate problem of how to make the railroads serve the national development of our resources. That means the fixing of rates so that railroads become available where they are most needed. Wastes and grafts have to be cut out, and the control of transportation made part of a national economic policy. You have to see to it that technical schools produce men trained for such work; you have to establish institutes of research, that shall stimulate the economic world not only with physical inventions, but with administrative proposals.

You have to go about deliberately to create a large class of professional business men. You have to enlarge the scope and the vision of the efficiency expert so that he can begin to take out of industry the deadening effects of machine production. You have to find vast sums of money for experiment in methods of humanizing labor.

For each industry you must discover the most satisfactory unit, and you must encourage these units to coöperate so that every industry shall be conducted with a minimum of friction. You must devise a banking system so that the nation's capital shall be available, that it shall be there for use at the lowest possible cost.

You have to find ways of making the worker an integral part of his industry. That means allowing him to develop his unions, and supplying the unions with every incentive by which they can increase their responsibility. You have to create an industrial education by which the worker shall be turned, not into an intelligent machine, but into an understanding, directing partner of business. You have to encourage the long process of self-education in democracy through which unions can develop representative government and adequate leadership. You have to support them in their desire to turn themselves from wage-earners into a corporate body that participates in industrial progress.

You have to devise and try out a great variety of consumers' controls. For some industries you may have to use public ownership, for others the coöperative society may be more effective, for others the regulating commission. You will not be able to come out plump for one method as against all the others. It will depend on the nature of the industry which instrument is the most effective. And back of all these methods, there is the need for industrial citizenship, for creating in the consumer a knowledge of what he wants, and of the different ways there are of getting it. Back of that there is the still subtler problem of making the consumer discriminating, of educating his taste and civilizing his desires.

All this is only a little of what has to be done. It has to be done not by some wise and superior being but by the American people themselves. No one man, no one group can possibly do it all. It is an immense collaboration. It will have to be carried out against the active opposition of class interests and sectional prejudices. At every step there will be a clash with old rights and old habits. There will be the cries of the beaten, the protest of the discarded. For men cling passionately to their routines.

But you cannot institute a better industrial order by decree. It is of necessity an educational process, a work of invention, of coöperative training, of battles against vested rights not only in property but in acquired skill as well, a process that is sure to be intricate, and therefore confusing.

But that is the way democracies move: they have in literal truth
to lift themselves by their own bootstraps. Those who have some
simpler method than the one I have sketched are, it seems to me,
either unaware of the nature of the problem, interested only in some
one phase of it, or unconsciously impatient with the limitations of
democracy. In the next chapter, I shall make an attempt to describe
some of the current philosophies which try to shirk the full force of
the problem. They are all excuses for trusting to luck, for relying
upon something but ourselves. They are all substitutes for the difficulties of self-government, concessions to the drift of our natures.

Here I want only to reach a sense of the complexity of the task,
its variety and its challenge. I have skimmed the surface, nothing
more. There is no mention of the fearful obstacles of race prejudice
in the South, no mention of the threat that recent immigration
brings with it, the threat of an alien and defenseless class of servile
labor. And there is, of course, always the distracting possibility of a
foreign war, of vast responsibilities in the other Americas.

Certainly democracy has a load to carry. It has arisen in the midst
of a civilization for which men are utterly unready, a civilization so
complex that their minds cannot grasp it, so unexpected that each
man is compelled to be something of a prophet. Its future is so uncertain that no one can feel any assurance in the face of it. Precedent
has been wrecked because we have to act upon really new facts.
Anything like a central authority to guide us has become impossible
because no authority is wise enough, because self-government has
become a really effective desire. The old shibboleths of conduct are
for the most part meaningless: they don't work when they are tried.

Through it all our souls have become disorganized, for they have
lost the ties which bound them. In the very period when man
most needs a whole-hearted concentration on external affairs, he is
disrupted internally by a revolution in the intimacies of his life.
He has lost his place in an eternal scheme, he is losing the ancient
sanctions of love, and his sexual nature is chaotic through the immense change that has come into the relations of parent and child,
husband and wife. Those changes distract him so deeply that the
more "advanced" he is, the more he flounders in the bogs of his
own soul.

9

Drift

It seems as if the most obvious way of reacting toward evil were to consider it a lapse from grace. The New Freedom, we are told, is "only the old revived and clothed in the unconquerable strength of modern America." Everywhere you hear it: that the people have been "deprived" of ancient rights, and legislation is framed on the notion that we can recover the alleged democracy of early America.

I once read in a learned magazine an essay on "The Oblivescence of the Disagreeable." As I remember it, the writer was trying to demonstrate what he regarded as a very hopeful truth —that men tend to forget pain more easily than pleasure. That is no doubt a comfortable faculty, but it plays havoc with history. For in regard to those early days of the Republic, most of our notions are marked by a well-nigh total oblivescence of the disagreeable. We find it very difficult to remember that there were sharp class divisions in the young Republic, that suffrage was severely restricted, that the Fathers were a very conscious upper class determined to maintain their privileges. Nations make their histories to fit their illusions. That is why reformers are so anxious to return to early America. What they know of it comes to them filtered through the golden lies of school-books and hallowed by the generous loyalty of their childhood.

Men generally find in the past what they miss in the present. During the Paterson strike of 1913, I heard a very drastic

I.W.W. agitator tell a meeting of silk-weavers that they had fallen low since the days of the great Chief Justice Marshall. In those days there were no rich and poor, and the Constitution had not yet been abrogated by an impudent Chief of Police! Yet in the days of Marshall even the most peaceful trade union was outlawed, and as for the doctrines of the I.W.W.,—imagine the sentiments of Alexander Hamilton. A few years ago I was living in Boston when an old gentleman, unhappy over the trend of democracy, published a book to glorify the American Tories. It consisted largely of intimate details from the private lives of the revolutionary heroes. Boston wouldn't have the book, true or untrue. So the old gentleman was denounced and his book forgotten.

For most of us insist that somewhere in the past there was a golden age. The modern puritan locates it in the period of the most famous ancestors from whom he can claim descent. That ancestor regretted the loss of Eden. Rousseau's millennial dream was a "state of nature." Hard-headed Adam Smith had his "original state" which was all that England wasn't. I know literary men who lament the passing of the eighteenth century coffee house, and New York is full of artists who dream of Parisian cafés. Zionists go back to David and Solomon; Celtic revivalists worry about Kathleen ni Houlihan; Chesterton dreams of Merrie England; scholars yearn for Fifth Century Athens; there is a considerable vogue to-day for certain of the earlier Egyptian dynasties, and some people, more radical than others, regard civilization itself as a disease.

The prototype of all revivals is each man's wistful sense of his own childhood. There is something infinitely pathetic in the way we persist in recalling what is by its very nature irrevocable. Perhaps each of us is touched by unuttered disappointments, and life has not the taste we anticipated. The weary man sinks back into the past, like a frightened child into its mother's arms. He glorifies what is gone when he fears what is to come. That is why discontented husbands have a way of admiring the cakes that mother used to bake. Beaten nations live in the exploits of their ancestors, and all exiles lament by the waters of Babylon. The curse of Ireland, of Poland, of Alsace is that they cannot forget what they were. There are no people who cling so ardently to a family tree as do those who have come down in the world. The men who were beaten by the trusts will never see the promise of the trusts.

Whenever the future is menacing and unfamiliar, whenever the day's work seems insurmountable, men seek some comfort in the warmth of memory. Only those who are really at home in their world find life more interesting as they mature. Experience for them is not an awful chance, but a prize they can win and embrace. They need no romance to make life tolerable. But people who are forever dreaming of a mythical past are merely saying that they are afraid of the future. They will falter before their problems, will deal with them half-heartedly and with diffidence. Their allegiance is not to the world. And they will never give themselves entirely to the task of making for themselves on this earth and in their age an adequate and civilized home.

The past which men create for themselves is a place where thought is unnecessary and happiness inevitable. The American temperament leans generally to a kind of mystical anarchism, in which the "natural" humanity in each man is adored as the savior of society. You meet this faith throughout the thousand and one communistic experiments and new religions in which America is so abundant. "If only you let men alone, they'll be good," a typical American reformer said to me the other day. He believed, as most Americans do, in the unsophisticated man, in his basic kindliness and his instinctive practical sense. A critical outlook seemed to the reformer an inhuman one; he distrusted, as Bryan does, the appearance of the expert; he believed that whatever faults the common man might show were due to some kind of Machiavellian corruption.

He had the American dream, which may be summed up, I think, in the statement that the undisciplined man is the salt of the earth. So when the trusts appeared, when the free land was gone, and America had been congested into a nation, the only philosophy with any weight of tradition behind it was a belief in the virtues of the spontaneous, enterprising, untrained and unsocialized man. Trust promoters cried: Let us alone. The little business men cried: We're the natural men, so let us alone. And the public cried: We're the most natural of all, so please do stop interfering with us. Muckraking gave an utterance to the small business men and to the larger public, who dominated reform politics. What did they do? They tried by all the machinery and power they could muster to restore a business world in which each man could again be left to his own will—a world that needed no coöperative intelligence. In the Sherman Act is symbolized this deliberate attempt to recreate an undeliberate society. No group of people, except the socialists, wished to take up the enormous task of disciplining business to popular need. For the real American was dreaming of the Golden Age in which he could drift with impunity.

But there has arisen in our time a large group of people who look to the future. They talk a great deal about their ultimate goal. Many of them do not differ in any essential way from those who dream of a glorious past. They put Paradise before them instead of behind them. They are going to be so rich, so great, and so happy some day, that any concern about to-morrow seems a bit sordid. They didn't fall from Heaven, as the reactionaries say, but they are going to Heaven with the radicals. Now this habit of reposing in the sun of a brilliant future is very enervating. It opens a chasm between fact and fancy, and the whole fine dream is detached from the living zone of the present. At the only point where effort and intelligence are needed, that point where to-day is turning into to-morrow, there these people are not found. At the point where human direction counts most they do not direct. So they are like most anarchists, wild in their dreams and unimportant in their deeds. They cultivate a castle in Spain and a flat in Harlem; a princess in the air and a drudge in the kitchen.

Then too there are the darlings of evolution. They are quite certain that evolution, as they put it, is ever onward and upward. For them all things conspire to achieve that well-known, though unmentioned far-off divine event to which the whole creation moves. They seem to imply as Moody[1] suggested:

> I, I, last product of the toiling ages,
>   Goal of heroic feet that never lagged,——

though

> A little thing in trousers, slightly jagged.

[1] The American poet William Vaughn Moody.

How the conservative goes to work with the idea of evolution has been ably exposed by William English Walling.[2] First, assume "progress" by calling it inevitable: this obviates the necessity for any practical change just now. Then assert the indubitable fact that real progress is very slow: and infer that wisdom consists in deprecating haste. Now when you have called progress inevitable and imperceptible, you have done about all that philosophy could do to justify impotence.

The radical view of evolution is more optimistic, but not more intelligent. In fact, it is generally all optimism and little else. For though it doesn't quite dare to say that whatever is, is right, it does assume that whatever is going to be, is going to be right. I believe that G. K. Chesterton once called this sort of thing progressivism by the calendar. There is complete confidence that whatever is later in time is better in fact, that the next phase is the desirable one, that all change is "upward," that God and Nature are collaborating in our blithe ascent to the Superman. Such an outlook undermines judgment and initiative, deliberate effort, invention, plan, and sets you adrift on the currents of time, hoping for impossible harbors.

In a constructive social movement the harm done is immeasurable. The most vivid illustration is that of the old-fashioned, fatalistic Marxian socialists. They have an implicit faith that human destiny is merely the unfolding of an original plan, some of the sketches of which are in their possession, thanks to the labors of Karl Marx. Strictly speaking, these men are not revolutionists as they believe themselves to be; they are the interested pedants of destiny. They are God's audience, and they know the plot so well that occasionally they prompt Him. In their system all that education, unions, leadership and thought can do is to push along what by the theory needs no pushing. These socialists are like the clown Marceline at the Hippodrome, who is always very busy assisting in labor that would be done whether he were there or not. They face the ancient dilemma of fatalism: whatever they do is right, and nothing they do

[2] The American Socialist, William English Walling, wrote some of the shrewdest critiques of American society and explanations of the nature of socialism: *Socialism As It Is* (New York: The Macmillan Company, 1912); *The Larger Aspects of Socialism* (New York: The Macmillan Company, 1913); and *Progressivism—and After* (New York: The Macmillan Company, 1914).

matters. Go to almost any socialist meeting and you'll hear it said that socialism would come if the Socialist Party had never been heard from. Perhaps so. But why organize a Socialist Party? Of course, socialists don't act upon their theory. They are too deeply impressed with the evil that exists, too eager for the future that they see, to trust entirely in the logic of events. They do try to shape that future. But their old fatalism hampers them enormously the moment any kind of action is proposed. They are out of sympathy with conservative trade unionism, but they are still more hostile to the I.W.W. In politics they despise the reformer, but when they themselves obtain office they do nothing that a hundred "bourgeois" reformers haven't done before them. The Socialist Party in this country has failed to develop a practical program for labor or a practical program for politics. It claims to have a different philosophy from that of trade unionists or reformers, but when you try to judge the difference by its concrete results, it is imperceptible.

The theory and the temper of orthodox socialism are fatalistic, and no fatalist can really give advice. Theory and practice are widely sundered in the American socialist movement. There is a stumbling revolt which lives from hand to mouth, a catch-as-catch-can struggle, and then far removed from it, standing in majesty, a great citadel of dogma almost impervious to new ideas. For in the real world, destiny is one of the aliases of drift.

Closely related in essence, though outwardly quite different, is what might be called the panacea habit of mind. Beginning very often in some penetrating insight or successful analysis, this sort of mind soon becomes incapable of seeing anything besides that portion of reality which sustains the insight and is subject to the analysis. A good idea, in short, becomes a fixed idea. One group of American socialists can see only the advantage of strikes, another of ballots. One reformer sees the advantages of the direct primaries in Wisconsin: they become the universal solvent of political evil. You find engineers who don't see why you can't build society on the analogy of a steam engine; you find lawyers, like Taft, who see in the courts an intimation of heaven; sanitation experts who wish to treat the whole world as one vast sanitarium; lovers who wish to treat it as one vast happy family; education enthusiasts who wish to treat it as one vast nursery. No one who undertook to be the Balzac of reform by writing its Human Comedy could afford to miss the way in which the reformer in each profession tends to make his specialty an analogy for the whole of life. The most amazing of all are people who deal with the currency question. Somehow or other, long meditation seems to produce in them a feeling that they are dealing with the crux of human difficulties.

Then there is the panacea most frequently propounded by voluble millionaires: the high cost of living is the cost of high living, and thrift is the queen of the virtues. Sobriety is another virtue, highly commended,—in fact there are thousands of people who seriously regard it as the supreme social virtue. To those of us who are sober and still discontented, the effort to found a political party on a colossal Don't is not very inspiring. After thrift and sobriety, there is always efficiency, a word which covers a multitude of confusions. No one in his senses denies the importance of efficient action, just as no one denies thrift and sober living. It is only when these virtues become the prime duty of man that we rejoice in the poet who has the courage to glorify the vagabond, preach a saving indolence, and glorify Dionysus. Be not righteous overmuch is merely a terse way of saying that virtue can defeat its own ends. Certainly, whenever a negative command like sobriety absorbs too much attention, and morality is obstinate and awkward, then living men have become cluttered in what was meant to serve them.

There are thousands to-day who, out of patience with almost everything, believe passionately that some one change will set everything right. In the first rank stand the suffragettes who believe that votes for women will make men chaste. I have just read a book by a college professor which announces that the short ballot will be as deep a revolution as the abolition of slavery. There are innumerable Americans who believe that a democratic constitution would create a democracy. Of course, there are single taxers so single-minded that they believe a happy civilization would result from the socialization of land values. Everything else that seems to be needed would follow spontaneously if only the land monopoly were abolished.

The syndicalists suffer from this habit of mind in an acute form. They refuse to consider any scheme for the reorganization of industry. All that will follow, they say, if only you can produce a General Strike. But obviously you might paralyze society, you might make the proletariat supreme, and still leave the proletariat without the slightest idea of what to do with the power it had won. What happens is that men gain some insight into society and concentrate their energy upon it. Then when the facts rise up in their relentless complexity, the only way to escape them is to say: Never mind, do what I advocate, and all these other things shall be added unto you.

There is still another way of reacting toward a too complicated world. That way is to see so much good in every reform that you can't make up your mind where to apply your own magnificent talents. The result is that you don't apply your talents at all.

Reform produces its Don Quixotes who never deal with reality; it produces its Brands who are single-minded to the brink of ruin; and it produces its Hamlets and its Rudins who can never make up their minds. What is common to them all is a failure to deal with the real world in the light of its possibilities. To try to follow all the aliases of drift is like attacking the hydra by cutting off its heads. The few examples given here of how men shirk self-government might be extended indefinitely. They are as common to radicals as to conservatives. You can find them flourishing in an orthodox church and among the most rebellious socialists.

Men will do almost anything but govern themselves. They don't want the responsibility. In the main, they are looking for some benevolent guardian, be it a "good man in office" or a perfect constitution, or the evolution of nature. They want to be taken in charge. If they have to think for themselves they turn either to the past or to a distant future: but they manage to escape the real effort of the imagination which is to weave a dream into the turning present. They trust to destiny, a quick one or a slow one, and the whole task of judging events is avoided. They turn to automatic devices: human initiative can be ignored. They forbid evil, and then they feel better. They settle on a particular analogy, or a particular virtue, or a particular policy, and trust to luck that everything else will take care of itself.

But no one of these substitutes for self-government is really satisfactory, and the result is that a state of chronic rebellion appears.

That is our present situation. The most hopeful thing about it is that through the confusion we can come to some closer understanding of why the modern man lacks stability, why his soul is scattered. We may, perhaps, be able to see a little better just what self-government implies.

The chronic rebellion is evident enough. I have a friend who after the Lawrence strike was a great admirer of the I.W.W. He told me about it one day with tears in his eyes. Two months later I met him, and he was cursing: "They're so successful that they're getting ready to throw So-and-So out of the I.W.W. for heresy." It is one of the ironies of the labor movement that it preaches solidarity, and seems to propagate by fission. For there is large truth in the saying that the only thing anarchists hate more than tyrants is an anarchist who differs with them. Indeed the bitterness between the "red" and the "yellow" unions is at least as great as the bitterness between the unions and the employers. The I.W.W. hates the American Federation of Labor and many political socialists with a vindictiveness that makes no distinction between them and the most tyrannical boss. Revolt within the world of revolt is an institution. If any capitalist thinks he is the object of abuse, he ought to come and hear a debate between the Detroit I.W.W. and the Chicago I.W.W.,[3] between believers in "direct" and in "political" action, between "State Socialists" and Syndicalists.

The sects of the rebellious are like the variety of the Protestant churches, and they are due to a similar cause. Once the churches had cut off from the deeply-rooted central tradition of Rome, they continued to cut off from each other. Now Protestantism was an effort at a little democracy in religion, and its history is amazingly like that of all the other revolts from the old absolutisms. For once men had broken loose from the cohesion and obedience of the older life, the floundering of democracy began. It was not so easy to become self governing as it was to bowl over a tyrant. And the long history of schisms is really the story of how men set up a substitute for authority, and had to revolt against it. To a man standing on

[3] Daniel De Leon, who headed the Detroit faction of the I.W.W., favored using political action to fight capitalism. The Chicago I.W.W., led by Vincent St. John and "Big Bill" Haywood, opposed political action and urged sabotage and direct action.

the firm foundation of an ancient faith, the instability of self-government is its just punishment, and no doubt he smiles at the folly of men who give up security and peace for a mess of revolt.

After Protestantism, the Romantic movement and the birth of political democracy. It is hardly necessary to recall what troubled spirits the romanticists were, how terrible the disillusionments. Their histories were with few exceptions tragic: and the "unending pursuit of the ever-fleeting object of desire" led many of them back into the arms of the Catholic Church. One has only to read the lives of the men whose names stand out in the nineteenth century to realize that the epoch of revolt produced tortured and driven spirits. Whatever their virtues, and they are many, they never attained that inner harmony whose outward sign is a cordial human life.

No one has felt this more poignantly than the modern artist. Lost in the clamor of commercialism, many painters seem to insist that if they can't make themselves admired they will at least make themselves heard. And of course, if you live in a world of studios, drawing-rooms and cafés, amidst idle people in little cliques, you have to draw attention to yourself from the outside world in some other way than by decorating or interpreting human life. The modern artist can secure attention, but he can't hold it. For the world is so complex that he can't find common experiences and common aspirations to deal with. And because he can't do this, he can't become artist to a nation. He has to be satisfied with a cult. So he specializes on some aspect of form, exaggerates some quality of line, and produces art that only a few people would miss if it disappeared. Then he denounces the philistine public.

But in his heart he is unsatisfied with his work, and so he too develops a habit of chronic rebellion: a school is no sooner founded when there is a secession. The usual manifesto is published (they all say about the same thing): authority and classicism are denounced in the name of youth and adventure. "All I want," said a friend of mine who paints, "is to bewilder and fascinate" . . . "All we need is wiggle," said another. "To be alive is to rebel," said a third. But I venture to suggest that what the rebels are rebelling against is not a classical authority: none exists to-day that has any compelling force. They are in rebellion against something within themselves; there are conflicts in their souls for which they have found no solution; and their revolt is the endless pursuit of what their own disharmony will never let them find.

> Nor certitude, nor peace, nor help for pain;
> And we are here as on a darkling plain
> Swept with confused alarms of struggle and flight,
> Where ignorant armies clash by night.

This certitude for which Matthew Arnold cries, where has it gone?

Classicists, like Prof. Babbitt of Harvard, or Mr. Paul Elmore More, say that it has gone with the shattering of external authority in the *débacle* of Romanticism and the French Revolution.[4] Their remedy for the chaos and ineptitude of modern life is a return to what they describe as eternal forms of justice and moderation. They would revive authority with its dominating critics like Boileau. Romanticism for them is a lapse from grace, full of sweet sin, and they hope to return to the Golden Age of the classics.

I don't see how this dream can succeed. Their solution is built on a wild impossibility, for in order to realize it they will have to abolish machinery and communication, newspapers and popular books. They will have to call upon some fairy to wipe out the memory of the last hundred years, and they will have to find a magician who can conjure up a church and a monarchy that men will obey. They can't do any of these things, though they can bewail the fact and display their grief by unremitting hostility to the modern world.

But though their remedy is, I believe, altogether academic, their diagnosis does locate the spiritual problem. We have lost authority. We are "emancipated" from an ordered world. We drift.

The loss of something outside ourselves which we can obey is a revolutionary break with our habits. Never before have we had to rely so completely upon ourselves. No guardian to think for us, no precedent to follow without question, no lawmaker above, only ordinary men set to deal with heart-breaking perplexity. All weakness comes to the surface. We are homeless in a jungle of machines

---

[4] Two of the chief critics of modernism, Professor Irving Babbitt of Harvard and Paul Elmer More of *The Nation*, attacked Romanticism and especially Rousseau's emphasis on the goodness of man.

and untamed powers that haunt and lure the imagination. Of course, our culture is confused, our thinking spasmodic, and our emotion out of kilter. No mariner ever enters upon a more uncharted sea than does the average human being born into the twentieth century. Our ancestors thought they knew their way from birth through all eternity: we are puzzled about the day after to-morrow.

What nonsense it is, then, to talk of liberty as if it were a happy-go-lucky breaking of chains. It is with emancipation that real tasks begin, and liberty is a searching challenge, for it takes away the guardianship of the master and the comfort of the priest. The iconoclasts didn't free us. They threw us into the water, and now we have to swim.

10

The Rock of Ages

I happened to be in Dublin some time ago during what was undoubtedly a crisis in Irish history: Home Rule in sight, Ulster arming itself for rebellion, Dublin torn by a bitter strike. No one felt any assurance as to the outcome. Before nationalism could prevail a long controversy seemed inevitable with the Presbyterian and industrial North. And even if Ireland became a nation it seemed as if it would have to face at once a sharp class struggle.

Then Mr. Hilaire Belloc arrived from England one evening to lecture before a Catholic Society. There seemed to be no doubts in Mr. Belloc's mind. He announced that his Church was the heir of all the arts and the guardian of all tradition. But the Catholic employers of Dublin, who were breaking up the workers' union with unparalleled bitterness, must have been somewhat puzzled by Mr. Belloc's statement. For in an issue of his paper two or three weeks before he had said with resounding conviction that the European tradition of Christendom always supported the rebellions of labor.

The same absolutism gave Mr. Belloc and the employers untroubled conviction, but the two convictions happened to be diametrically opposed. Neither side suffered from the malady of doubt, the employers being ready to defy the temporal law by locking up the men's leaders; the men ready to defy the laws of property by throwing packing-cases into the river Liffey.

Now this is the peculiar fact about an absolute faith: that while it makes a man *feel* sure of himself, it doesn't enable him to be sure. Mr. Belloc in his untroubled way felt certain about events that in plain fact were full of uncertainty. It was all very well to say in cocksure fashion that Christian tradition was this-and-that. Christian employers, Christian priests, Christian newspapers made it something else. But human beings seem to be made in such a way that they cling passionately to the emotion of certainty. If only they can retain the feeling that God and Nature and history are with them, they go about with every appearance of conviction and practical power. They have far less bother about their souls than the modern man lost in a fog of introspection. For the believer in an absolute system has projected upon the world that certainty and harmony which he needs. His difficulties after that are merely matters of detail. The massive structure of his faith will dwarf the puny evidence of fact. And so, freed from doubts as to the eternal principles of truth and righteousness, he can give undivided attention to ordinary events. Do not wonder then at the practical efficiency of mystics, the executive genius of priests and cardinals, and the shrewdness of those who profess an unworldly religion. If the genuine interests of man lie beyond this earth, why exhibit such marvelous competence about the things which the moths eat and the dust corrupts? That's a good question for a debater, but not for a student of men. Belief does not live by logic, but by the need it fills, and absolutism quiets the uncertainties of the soul, finds answers to unsatisfied desire, and endows men with the sense that they are part of something greater than themselves. In the worldly power of the Roman Church, of Christian Science, of the Salvation Army, or the Mormons, you come to see what a colossal, practical power there is in an untroubled faith. But in liberal thought there is chaos, for it lacks the foundations of certainty.

Now when a man is looking for something really trustworthy he is likely to think of something solid, like a rock. Gibraltar has always been an excellent symbol of the qualities a man hopes to find in his insurance companies. And those qualities, you can rest assured, are the ones with which he would like to insure his destiny. For real comfort, give a man a world that will stand still, that will be the same to-morrow as it was yesterday, so that no matter how much he is buffeted about, there will be one place he can go and not be surprised. The mother is such a refuge to a bewildered child, and Mother Church has been that to her bewildered children. We are none of us progressives when we are worried or tired; few of us are revolutionists in a personal crisis. We have to be very healthy to love variety. We have to be exuberant and conquering to rejoice in change. And that I imagine is why man has always attached such high emotional value to the One, the All Embracing, the Permanent. There are people who flatly refuse to regard Pluralism as a philosophy of life. William James recognized that and spent a large amount of time trying to show that a disorderly world full of variety and spontaneous creation might still give religious satisfaction. I doubt whether he succeeded. The only people who can stomach a pluralistic philosophy are those who in some way or another have grown strong enough to do without an absolute faith.

It has often been said that the Catholic Church is the greatest piece of constructive psychology that the world has ever seen. Certainly it would be hard to duplicate the ingenious answers it has found to human need: the cavernous mysteries of its cathedrals converging upon the enduring altar, the knowledge of an Eternal Family that survives the human one, the confessional where sin could be expressed and therefore purged, the vicarious atonement by which the consequences of human weakness were lifted off men's shoulders, the obliteration of death, the sense that wisdom was there inexhaustible and infallible. Those aren't idle dogmas, as foolish critics have imagined, but endlessly ingenious responses to the everyday wants of men and women. And then the invariable presence of the Church at every important crisis in human life—at birth, at puberty, at marriage, on the battlefield, at the death-bed,—wherever men were troubled and in need of help, there the Church was to be found. So men might forget the Church in their prosperity but in sorrow they returned to it. Of course, the Church was no aid to the inventor or to anyone who was really extending the bounds of human power. Of course, it was hostile to democracy and to every force that tended to make people self-sufficient.

In fact, the Church was not content to meet needs and compensate weakness. It tried to make weakness permanent. In other words, the Church used all its tremendous power over men to keep them wanting that which the Church could give. "What is your age? Is it twenty, thirty, forty, or are you still older? . . . Death will take from you the future, as it took from you the past, with the rapidity of lightning . . . To die . . . is to go . . . where you will become the prey of corruption and the food of the most hideous reptiles." This is from the "First Exercise on Death" in the Spiritual Exercises of St. Ignatius. Take this from the Third Exercise: "Consider—1. A few moments after your death. Your body laid on a funeral bed, wrapped in a shroud, a veil thrown over your face; beside you the crucifix, the holy water, friends, relatives, a priest kneeling by your sad remains, and reciting the holy prayers, 'De profundis clamvi ad te, Domine'; the public officer who writes in the register of the dead all the particulars of your decease."

In the lovely little book from which I am quoting this kind of thing is recommended for daily contemplation, a capital way, it seems to me, of poisoning the human will. It was this that Nietzsche had in mind when he said that "belief is always most desired, most pressingly needed where there is a lack of will—the less a person knows how to command, the more urgent is his desire for one who commands sternly,—a God, a prince, a caste, a physician, a confessor, a dogma, a party conscience."

Yet a stern commander is just what this age lacks. Liberalism suffuses our lives and the outstanding fact is the decay of authority. But this doesn't mean for one minute that we are able to command ourselves. In fact, if a man dare attempt to sum up the spiritual condition of his time, he might say of ours that it has lost authority and retained the need of it. We are freer than we are strong. We have more responsibility than we have capacity. And if we wish to state what the future sets for us, we might say, I think, that we must find within ourselves the certainty which the external world has lost.

It is not fair to claim that we who attack absolutism are robbing life of its guarantees. It is far truer to say that the enlargement and ferment of the modern world have robbed absolutism of its excuse. To the business man who believes sincerely in the old sanctities of private property, the industrial situation must seem like a mine of explosives. The legalist gasps in panic. And as for these new aspirations of women, this push of the working-class towards an industrial democracy, this faculty of the young for taking an interest in life uncensored, what lamp-post is there that a man can embrace in a giddy and reeling universe? None. It was possible to talk about eternal principles of conduct in an old-world village where the son replaced the father generation after generation, where the only immigrants were babies and the only emigrants the dead. But in the new world, where fifty races meet, and a continent is exploited, ten years is an enormous change, a generation is a revolution.

Life has overflowed the little systems of eternity. Thought has become humbler because its task is greater. We can invoke no monumental creeds, because facts smile ironically upon them. And so in a changing world, men have to cast aside the old thickset forms of their thinking for suppler experimental ones. They think oftener. They think more lavishly, and they don't hang their hope of immortality on the issue of their thoughts. It is not so comfortable. It gives none of that harmony outside which men desire. The challenge is endless, to finer perceptions and sharper insights. Such thinking is more accurate than settled principles can ever be; the restless modern world has made such thinking necessary. But gone are the repose and the sublimity and the shelter of larger creeds. Our thought is homely, of the earth, and not awe-inspiring. No profound homage can go out to ideas that an honest man may have to scrap to-morrow. There is nothing of Gibraltar about to-day's hypothesis.

The most dramatic revelation of this crisis is among the newer immigrants in an American city. They come suddenly from the fixed traditions of peasant life into the distracting variety of a strange civilization. America for them is not only a foreign country where they have to find a living in ways to which they are unaccustomed; America is a place where their creeds do not work, where what at home seemed big and emphatic as the mountains is almost unnoticed. It is a commonplace to say that the tide of emigration has shifted from the Northwest to the Southeast of Europe, and that America to-day is receiving a radically different stock than it did twenty years ago. That is undoubtedly true. But the difference is not only in the immigrants. America itself is different. Those who are coming to-day have to bridge a much greater gap than did those who entered this country when it was a nation of villages.

They come to a country which shatters cynically the whole structure of their emotional life. There is a brave attempt to preserve it in ghettos. But with no great success, and the second generation is drawn unprotected into the new world. Parents and children often hardly understand each others' speech, let alone each others' desires.

In Queenstown harbor I once talked to an Irish boy who was about to embark for America. His home was in the West of Ireland, in a small village where his sister and he helped their father till a meager farm. They had saved enough for a passage to America, and they were abandoning their home. I asked the boy whether he knew anyone in America. He didn't, but his parish priest at home did. He was going to write to Father Riley every week. Would he ever return to Ireland? "Yes," said this boy of eighteen, "I'm going to die in Ireland." Where was he going to in America? To a place called New Haven. He was, in short, going from one epoch into another, and for guidance he had the parish priest at home and perhaps the ward boss in New Haven. His gentleness and trust in the slums of New Haven, assaulted by din and glare, hedged in by ugliness and cynical push,—if there is any adventure comparable to his, I have not heard of it. At the very moment when he needed a faith, he was cutting loose from it. If he becomes brutal, greedy, vulgar, will it be so surprising? If he fails to measure up to the requirements of citizenship in a world reconstruction, is there anything strange about it?

Well, he was an immigrant in the literal sense. All of us are immigrants spiritually. We are all of us immigrants in the industrial world, and we have no authority to lean upon. We are an uprooted people, newly arrived, and *nouveau riche*. As a nation we have all the vulgarity that goes with that, all the scattering of soul. The modern man is not yet settled in his world. It is strange to him, terrifying, alluring, and incomprehensibly big. The evidence is everywhere: the amusements of the city; the jokes that pass for jokes; the blare that stands for beauty, the folksongs of Broadway, the feeble and apologetic pulpits, the cruel standards of success, raucous purity. We make love to ragtime and we die to it. We are blown hither and thither like litter before the wind. Our days are lumps of undigested experience. You have only to study what newspapers regard as news to see how we are torn and twisted by the irrelevant:

in frenzy about issues that do not concern us, bored with those that do. Is it a wild mistake to say that the absence of central authority has disorganized our souls, that our souls are like Peer Gynt's onion, in that they lack a kernel?

Part Three

11

A Note on the Woman's Movement

Liberty may be an uncomfortable blessing unless you know what to do with it. That is why so many freed slaves returned to their masters, why so many emancipated women are only too glad to give up the racket and settle down. For between announcing that you will live your own life, and the living of it lie the real difficulties of any awakening.

If all that women needed were "rights,"—the right to work, the right to vote, and freedom from the authority of father and husband, then feminism would be the easiest human question on the calendar. For while there will be a continuing opposition, no one supposes that these elementary freedoms can be withheld from women. In fact, they will be forced upon millions of women who never troubled to ask for any of these rights. And that isn't because Ibsen wrote the Doll's House, or because Bernard Shaw writes prefaces. The mere withdrawal of industries from the home has drawn millions of women out of the home, and left millions idle within it. There are many other forces, all of which have blasted the rock of ages where woman's life was centered. The self-conscious modern woman may insist that she has a life of her own to lead, which neither father, nor priest, nor husband, nor Mrs. Grundy is fit to prescribe for her. But when she begins to prescribe life for herself, her real problems begin.

Every step in the woman's movement is creative. There are no precedents whatever, not even bad ones. Now the invention of new ways of living is rare enough among men, but among women it has been almost unknown. Housekeeping and baby-rearing are the two most primitive arts in the whole world. They are almost the last occupations in which rule of thumb and old wives' tales have resisted the application of scientific method. They are so immemorially backward, that nine people out of ten hardly conceive the possibility of improving upon them. They are so backward that we have developed a maudlin sentimentality about them, have associated family life and the joy in childhood with all the stupidity and wasted labor of the inefficient home. The idea of making the home efficient will cause the average person to shudder, as if you were uttering some blasphemy against monogamy. "Let science into the home, where on earth will Cupid go to?" Almost in vain do women like Mrs. Gilman[1] insist that the institution of the family is not dependent upon keeping woman a drudge amidst housekeeping arrangements inherited from the early Egyptians. Women have invented almost nothing to lighten their labor. They have made practically no attempt to specialize, to coöperate. They have been the great routineers.

So people have said that woman was made to be the natural conservative, the guardian of tradition. She would probably still be guarding the tradition of weaving her own clothes in the parlor if an invention hadn't thwarted her. She still guards the tradition of buying food retail, of going alone and unorganized to market. And she has been, of course, a faithful conservator of superstition, the most docile and credulous of believers. In all this, I am saying nothing that awakened women themselves aren't saying, nor am I trying to take a hand in that most stupid of all debates as to whether men are superior to women. Nor am I trying to make up my mind whether the higher education of women and their political enfranchisement will produce in the next generation several Darwins and a few Michelangelos. The question is not even whether women can be as good doctors and lawyers and business organizers as men.

It is much more immediate, and far less academic than that. The

[1] The outspoken feminist leader Mrs. Charlotte (Perkins) Stetson Gilman wrote *Women and Economics* (Boston: Small, Maynard, 1898); *In This Our World* (Boston: Small, Maynard, 1898); *Human Work* (New York: McClure, Phillips, 1904); *What Diantha Did* (New York: Charlton, 1910); and *The Man-made World* (New York: Charlton, 1911).

feminists could almost afford to admit the worst that Schopenhauer, Weininger, and Sir Almoth Wright[2] can think of, and then go on pointing to the fact that competent or incompetent they have got to adjust themselves to a new world. The day of the definitely marked "sphere" is passing under the action of forces greater than any that an irritated medical man can control. It is no longer possible to hedge the life of women in a set ritual, where their education, their work, their opinion, their love, and their motherhood, are fixed in the structure of custom. To insist that women need to be moulded by authority is a shirking of the issue. For the authority that has moulded them is passing. And if woman is fit only to live in a harem, it will have to be a different kind of harem from any that has existed.

The more you pile up the case against woman in the past the more significant does feminism become. For one fact is written across the whole horizon, the prime element in any discussion. That fact is the absolute necessity for a readjusting of woman's position. And so, every time you insist that women are backward you are adding to the revolutionary meaning of their awakening. But what these anti-feminists have in mind, of course, is that women are by nature incapable of any readjustment. However, the test of that pudding is in the eating. What women will do with the freedom that is being forced upon them is something, that no person can foresee by thinking of women in the past.

Women to-day are embarked upon a career for which their tradition is no guide. The first result, of course is a vast amount of trouble. The emancipated woman has to fight something worse than the crusted prejudices of her uncles; she has to fight the bewilderment in her own soul. She who always took what was given to her has to find for herself. She who passed without a break from the dominance of her father to the dominance of her husband is suddenly compelled to govern herself. Almost at one stroke she has lost the authority of a little world and has been thrust into a very big one, which nobody, man or woman, understands very well. I have tried

[2] The deeply pessimistic nineteenth-century German philosopher Arthur Schopenhauer viewed women as ugly, perverse, and mindless. Otto Weininger was the author of *Geschlecht und charakter* (1903), first published in English as *Sex and Character* in 1906. Sir Almoth Wright wrote *The Unexpurgated Case against Woman Suffrage* (1913).

to suggest what this change from a world of villages has meant for politicians, clergymen and social thinkers. Well, for women, the whole problem is aggravated by the fact that they come from a still smaller world and from a much more rigid authority.

It is no great wonder if there is chaos among the awakening women. Take a cry like that for a "single standard" of morality. It means two utterly contradictory things. For the Pankhursts[3] it is assumed that men should adopt women's standards, but in the minds of thousands it means just the reverse. For some people feminism is a movement of women to make men chaste, for others the enforced chastity of women is a sign of their slavery. Feminism is attacked both for being too "moral" and too "immoral." And these contradictions represent a real conflict, not a theoretical debate. There is in the movement an uprising of women who rebel against marriage which means to a husband the ultimate haven of a sexual career. There is also a rebellion of women who want for themselves the larger experience that most men have always taken. Christabel Pankhurst uses the new freedom of expression to drive home an Old Testament morality with Old Testament fervor. She finds her book suppressed by Mr. Anthony Comstock, who differs from her far less than he imagines. And she rouses the scorn of great numbers of people who feel that she is out, not to free women, but to enslave men. There is an immense vacillation between a more rigid Puritanism and the idolatry of freedom. Women are discovering what reformers of all kinds are learning, that there is a great gap between the overthrow of authority and the creation of a substitute. That gap is called liberalism: a period of drift and doubt. We are in it to-day.

The first impulse of emancipation seems to be in the main that woman should model her career on man's. But she cannot do that for the simple reason that she is a woman. Towards love and children her attitude is not man's, as everyone but a doctrinaire knows. She cannot taboo her own character in order to become suddenly an amateur male. And if she could, it would be the sheerest folly, for there are plenty of men on this earth.

Yet at the very time when enlightened people are crying out against the horrors of capitalism, you will find many feminists

[3] The Pankhursts were the leaders of the militant British suffragettes.

urging women to enter capitalism as a solution of their problems. Of course, millions have been drawn in against their will, but there is still a good number who go in voluntarily, because they feel that their self-respect demands it.

They go in response to the desire for economic independence. And they find almost no real independence in the industrial world. What has happened, it seems to me, is this: the women who argue for the necessity of making one's own living are almost without exception upper class women, either because they have special talents or because they have special opportunities. Some time ago I attended a feminist meeting where a brilliant woman was presented to the audience as an example of how it was possible to earn a living and have twins at the same time. But it happened that the woman was a lecturer who could earn a very comfortable sum by speaking a few hours a week. Another woman at the same meeting was an actress, another had been a minister, another was a popular novelist; the only woman present who was concerned with factory work said not one word about the pleasure of earning your own living.

Now, only a very small percentage of men or women can enter the professions. For the great mass, economic independence means going to work. And the theorists of feminism have yet to make up their minds whether they can seriously urge women to go into industry as it is to-day or is likely to be in the near future. I, for one, should say that the presence of women in the labor market is an evil to be combatted by every means at our command. The army of women in industry to-day is not a blessing but the curse of a badly organized society. Their position there is not the outpost of an advance toward a fuller life but an outrage upon the race, and I believe that the future will regard it as a passing phase of human servitude.

For the great mass, women's work in the future will, I believe, be in the application of the arts and sciences to a deepened and more extensively organized home. There is nothing narrowing about that, no thrusting of women back into the chimney corner. There is opportunity for every kind of talent, and for the sharing of every kind of interest. It does not mean that women need not concern themselves with industry. Far from it. For any decent kind of home women will have to develop beyond anything we have to-day an intelligent and powerful consumers' control. They must go into politics, of course, for no home exists that doesn't touch in a hundred ways upon the government of cities, states and the nation. They have the whole educational system to deal with, not only from the public school up, but also, what is beginning to be recognized as most important of all, from infancy to school age. Nor does it mean that every women must be an incompetent amateur of all the arts, as she is today, a cook, a purchaser, a housekeeper, a trained nurse and a kindergarten teacher. Woman's work can and will be specialized, as Mrs. Gilman has pointed out, so that a woman will have a very wide choice in a host of new careers that are going to be created. A great many things which are done in each house will be done by the collective action of a group of houses. The idea of having forty kitchens, forty furnaces, forty laundries, and forty useless backyards in one square block, managed by forty separate overworked women, each going helplessly to market, each bringing up children by rule of thumb,—all that is a kind of individualism which the world will get away from.

To get away from it is an effort that will provide ample careers for most women. The elementary facts of coöperation and division of labor are being forced upon women by the wastefulness of the old kind of housekeeping. We see already the organization of housewives' associations, of common playgrounds, which some people object to when they have a roof and are called common nurseries. There are neighborhood associations, and women's municipal leagues. There are kindergartens which take away from each mother the necessity of being an accomplished teacher of the most subtly plastic period of human life.

Now with the development of some division of labor among women, they will begin to earn salaries. To be paid for work in money is possible only when you don't do all the work. So the moment you divide the work the only way you can share the product is by paying money to each worker. A woman who does her own cooking gets no pay. A woman who does someone else's cooking gets pay. And when women introduce into the work of the home the principle of division of labor and coöperative organization, they also will receive pay, and what is called "economic independence" will be open to them. That will, of course, be a real emancipation. If women are trained to do all the things that the existing home requires, that is, if they become amateur cooks, marketers, and Montessori mothers, and specialists in none of these things, then they have to wait till they can have a home of their own in which to display their versatility. They have to wait for a man who loves them enough to put up with their general amateurishness, or one who doesn't know any better. But the moment they specialize, so that women can do some one thing very well, they can begin to do homework before they are married. A kindergarten teacher doesn't have to bear a child before she can begin to teach a child. She has a place in the world, a livelihood, and a self-respect because she can do something which is needed. She can marry for love, because she desires children of her own, because she wants what the family can give, not because she is a detached and meaningless female until she is married.

What this will mean for everyone is almost beyond the imagination of most people to-day. We are just beginning to realize that the intense narrowness of women is one of the things that thwarts human effort. The number of wives who have egged their husbands on to ruthless business practices, the inventive minds that have been stunted by a fierce absorption in the little interests of the household—all the individualism of women is a constant obstacle to a larger coöperative life. If we knew the details of why men falter, why they are pulled away from common action, we should find, I believe, in unnumbered cases that there was some woman at home, a mother or a wife, who, limited in her whole vision, was clinging desperately to some immediate, personal advantage. And as for children, in their most educable period, they are surrounded by an example of isolation, made to feel that the supreme concern of human life is to look in towards the home, instead of out from it. It is no wonder that democracy is so difficult, that collective action is impeded by a thousand conflicting egotisms. Every one of us is trained in a little water-tight compartment of his own.

From the economic and spiritual subjection of his mother the child forms its ideal of the relation of men and women. We speak about the influence of the parents. It is deeper than most of us realize. The child is influenced by its parents, but not only for good, as sentimentalists seem to imagine. The boy may absorb all the admirable qualities of his father, but he is just as capable of absorbing his father's contempt for woman's mind, his father's capacity for playing the little tyrant, and his father's bad economic habits. The girl learns to obey, to wait on the lordly male, to feel unimportant in human affairs, to hold on with unremitting force to the privileges that sex gives her. And out of it all we get the people of to-day, unused to the very meaning of democracy, grasping their own with an almost hysterical tenacity.

The sense of property may be a deep instinct. But surely the nineteenth century home stimulated that instinct to the point of morbidity. For it did almost nothing to bring the child into contact with the real antidote to acquisitiveness—a sense of social property. To own things in common is, it seems to me, one of the most educating experiences in the world. Those people who can feel that they possess the parks, the libraries, the museums of their city, are likely to be far more civilized people than those who want a park which they can enclose, and who want to own a masterpiece all by themselves. It is well known that there is among sea-faring people a rare comradeship. May this not be due to the fact that the sea is there for all to use and none to own? On the high road men salute each other in passing. Farmers seem at times to have a kind of personal friendship with the weather and the turning seasons, and those things which no single man can appropriate.

Now in the complicated civilization upon which we are entering, it will be impossible for many people to enjoy the primitive sense of absolute possession. We shall need men and women who can take an interest in collective property, who can feel personally and vividly about it. One of the great promises of the conservation movement is the evidence it gave of a passionate attachment to public possessions. But that attachment is something that almost everyone to-day has had to acquire after he was grown up. We are all of us compelled to overcome the habits and ideals of a childhood where social property was almost unknown. In this respect the only child is perhaps the most deeply miseducated. He has had what he had as his in fee simple. But all children have far too little contact with other children—too few toys that are owned in common, too few group nurseries. Now boys, when they grow to be a bit older, do come in for a little social education. The gang is a fine experience, even though a few windows are smashed. The boy who can talk about "us fellers" has a better start for the modern world than the little girl of the same age who is imitating her mother's housekeeping. From the gang to the athletic team, class spirit, school spirit —with all their faults and misdirected energy—they do mean loyalty to something larger than the petty details of the moment.

One of the supreme values of feminism is that it will have to socialize the home. When women seek a career they have to specialize. When they specialize they have to coöperate. They have to abandon more and more the self-sufficient individualism of the older family. They will have to market through associations. They will do a great deal more of the housework through associations, just as they are now beginning to have bread baked outside and the washing done by laundries that are not part of the home. If they are not satisfied with the kind of work that is done for the home but outside of it, they will have to learn that difficult business of democracy which consists in expressing and enforcing their desires upon industry. And just as from the kindergarten up, education has become a collective function, so undoubtedly a great deal of the care and training of infants will become specialized.

This doesn't mean baby-farms or barracks or any of the other nightmares of the hysterical imagination. Nobody is proposing to separate the child from its parents any more than the child is now separated. It is curious how readily any woman who can afford it will trust her infant to the most ignorant nurse-girl, and then be horribly shocked at the idea of trusting her child to day nurseries in charge of trained women. The private nurse-girl often abuses the child in unmentionable ways, but she is preferred because she seems somehow to satisfy the feeling of possession. The penalty that grown-ups pay for the sins of the superstitious and unsocialized nursery is something that we are just beginning to understand from the researches of the psychiatrists.

There is one question about feminism which is sure to have risen in the mind of any reader who has followed the argument up to this point. Does the awakening of women mean an attack upon monogamy? For the moment anyone dares to criticize any arrangement of the existing home he might as well be prepared to find himself classed as a sexual anarchist. It is curious how little faith conservatives have in the institution of the family. They will tell you how deep it is in the needs of mankind, and they will turn around and act as if the home were so fragile that collapse would follow the first whiff of criticism.

Now I believe that the family *is* deeply grounded in the needs of mankind, or it would never survive the destructive attacks made upon it, not by radical theorists, mind you, but by social conditions. At the present moment over half the men of the working-class do not earn enough to support a family, and that's why their wives and their daughters are drawn into industry. The family survives that, men and women do still want to marry and have children. But we put every kind of obstacle in their way. We pay such wages that young men can't afford to marry. We do not teach them the elementary facts of sex. We allow them to pick up knowledge in whispered and hidden ways. We surround them with the tingle and glare of cities, stimulate them, and then fall upon them with a morality which shows no quarter. We support a large class of women in idleness, the soil in which every foolish freak can flourish. We thrust people into marriage and forbid them with fearful penalties to learn any way of controlling their own fertility. We do almost no single, sensible, and deliberate thing to make family life a success. And still the family survives.

It has survived all manner of stupidity. It will survive the application of intelligence. It will not collapse because the home is no longer the scene of drudgery and wasted labor or because children are reared to meet modern civilization. It will not collapse because women have become educated, or because they have attained a new self-respect.

But in answer to the direct question whether monogamy is to go by the board, the only possible answer is this: there is no reason for supposing that there will be any less of it than there is to-day. That is not saying very much, perhaps, but more than that no honest person can guarantee. He can believe that when the thousand irritations of married life are reduced, the irritations of an unsound economic status, of ignorance in the art of love, then the family will have a better chance than it has ever had. How many homes have been wrecked by the sheer inability of men and women to understand each other can be seen by the enormous use made of the theme in modern literature. It does not seem to me that education and a growing sensitiveness are likely to make for promiscuity.

For you have to hold yourself very cheaply to endure the appalling and unselective intimacy that promiscuity means. To treat women as things and yourself as a predatory animal is the product not of emancipation and self-respect, but of ignorance and inferiority. The uprising of women as personalities is not likely to make them value themselves less, nor is it likely that they will be satisfied with the fragments of love they now attain. Of course, every movement attracts what Roosevelt calls its "lunatic fringe," and feminism has collected about it a great rag-tag of bohemianism. But it cannot be judged by that; it must be judged by its effect on the great mass of women who, half-consciously for the most part, are seeking not a new form of studio and café life, but a readjustment to work and love and interest. There is among them, so far as I can see, no indication of any desire for an impressionistic sexual career.

To be sure they don't treat a woman who has had relations out of marriage as if she were a leper. They are not inclined to visit upon the offspring of illegitimacy the curse of patriarchal Judæa. But so far as their own demands go they are set in overwhelming measure upon greater sexual sincerity. They are, if anything, too stern in their morality and, perhaps, too naïve. But the legislation they initiate, the books they write, look almost entirely to the establishment of a far more enduring and intelligently directed family.

The effect of the woman's movement will accumulate with the generations. The results are bound to be so far-reaching that we can hardly guess them to-day. For we are tapping a reservoir of possibilities when women begin to use not only their generalized womanliness but their special abilities. For the child it means, as I have tried to suggest, a change in the very conditions where the property sense is aggravated and where the need for authority and individual assertiveness is built up. The greatest obstacles to a cooperative civilization are under fire from the feminists. Those obstacles today are more than anything else a childhood in which the anti-social impulses are fixed. The awakening of women points straight to the discipline of coöperation. And so it is laying the real foundations for the modern world.

For understand that the forms of coöperation are of precious little value without a people trained to use them. The old family with its dominating father, its submissive and amateurish mother produced inevitably men who had little sense of a common life, and women who were jealous of an enlarging civilization. It is this that feminism comes to correct, and that is why its promise reaches far beyond the present bewilderment.

12

Bogeys

There are people who are always waiting for the heavens to fall. In 1879, when Massachusetts granted school suffrage to women, a legislator arose and said: "If we make this experiment we shall destroy the race, which will be blasted by Almighty God." That silly man was not a prehistoric specimen. He is always with us. And he is in the soul of most of us. He is the panic that seized Chicago over the Haymarket anarchists; he is what makes preachers cry out that the tango is wrecking the nation; he is the white slave legend; he is Mr. Taft contemplating the recall of judges.

I know how bogeys are made. I was a child of four during the panic of '93, and Cleveland has always been a sinister figure to me. His name was uttered with monstrous dread in the household. Then came Bryan, an ogre from the West, and a waiting for the election returns of 1896 with beating heart. And to this day I find myself with a subtle prejudice against Democrats that goes deeper than what we call political conviction.

I can remember a birthday "party" for two or three chums which developed into a "rough-house." In the excitement we used cakes as ammunition, leaving the carpet in a shocking state. This angered the maid who was responsible for the tidiness of my room to such a pitch that only religion seemed adequate for the occasion. In the late afternoon she began to talk to me in a solemn voice. I would have preferred a thousand beatings to that voice in the wretched gaslight which used to darken homes before electricity reached the middle-class. The flickering shadows on the cake-strewn carpet were unbearable and accusing shapes full of foreboding to boys lost in sin. I burst into tears at the impending wrath of God. And for years God was the terror of the twilight.

With that somehow or other was associated a belief that the world was about to come to an end. I think the nurse had read the predictions of some astronomer in a newspaper, and the news was communicated to me. It became part of the twilight, and was mixed up with thunderstorms, and going into a dark room. Then too, there were ghosts, but I laid them one night after everyone had gone to bed in what is undoubtedly the most heroic exploit of my life. I still glow with pride in the telling. I got out of bed and turned on the light, identified the ghost with the lace curtain, went back to bed, turned on the light once more, made sure that the ghost *was* the curtain, and felt immeasurably happier.

Generally, however, we create the bogey by pulling the bedclothes over our heads. A friend of mine couldn't be cured of his socialist phobia until he happened one day to see the most terrible agitator of them all buying a pair of suspenders. For in the seclusion and half-light of class tradition and private superstitution, in a whispered and hesitant atmosphere, phantoms thrive. But in direct contact by an unromantic light evil is no longer a bogey but a problem. That is the way to approach evil: by stating it and manhandling it: the fevered gloom subsides, for that gloom does not belong to evil; it it is merely the feeling of a person who is afraid of evil. "Death," said a wise man, "is not feared because it is evil, but it is evil because it is feared."

To overcome the subjective terrors: that is an important aspect of the age-long struggle out of barbarism. Romantic persons like to paint savages as care-free poets living in thoughtless happiness from day to day. Nothing could be further from the facts. The life of a savage is beset by glowering terrors: from birth to death he lives in an animated world; where the sun and the stars, sticks, stones, and rivers are obsessed with his fate. He is busy all the time in a ritual designed to propitiate the abounding jealousies of nature. For his world is magical and capricious, the simplest thing is occult. In that atmosphere there is no possibility of men being able to face their life without heroics and without terror, simply and gladly. They need authority: they need to be taken in charge; they cannot trust themselves.

That is why the exorcising of bogeys is so intimate a part of the effort at self-government. Think of the ordinary business man's notion of an anarchist, or the anarchist's notion of a business man; many men's feeling about Theodore Roosevelt, or Bill Haywood, or the Capitalist Class, or the Money Power, or Sex Reform—I use capital letters because these fantasies have become terrific monsters of the imagination. Our life is overwrought with timidities and panics, distorting superstitutions and fantastic lures: our souls are misshapen by the plucking of invisible hands.

The regiment of bogeys is waiting for people at birth, where the cruellest unreason clusters about illegitimacy. It attacks the young child who asks how he was born. For answer he is given lies and a sense of shame; for ever afterwards he too lies and is ashamed. And so we begin to build up the sense of sin and the furtiveness of sex. The body becomes the object of a sneaking curiosity, of a tingling and embarrassing interest. We surround the obvious with great wastes of silence, and over the simplest facts we teach the soul to stutter.

What we call purity is not honest and temperate desire, but a divided life in which our "Better Nature" occasionally wins a bankrupt victory. Children are immured in what their parents fondly picture to be a citadel of innocence. In reality, they are plunged into fantastic brooding or into a haphazard education. Behind innocence there gathers a clotted mass of superstition, of twisted and misdirected impulse; clandestine flirtation, fads, and ragtime fill the unventilated mind.

Then too the whole edifice of class-feeling—what "is done" and what "isn't done," and who are "the best people" and who are the "impossible," and sleepless nights over whether you were correctly dressed, or whether you will be invited to be seen with Mrs. So-and-So. It makes sheep out of those who conform and freaks out of those who rebel. Every fairly intelligent person is aware that the price of respectability is a muffled soul bent on the trivial and the mediocre. The mere fact that the weight of custom is on the accidents of class is a tremendous item in the lives of those who try to live in a human sphere. No one escapes the deformity altogether. Certainly not the modern rebel. His impulse is to break away from the worship of idols to central human values. But the obstruction of class feeling is so great that he becomes a kind of specialist in rebellion. He is so busy asserting that he isn't conventional that the easy, natural humanity he professes to admire is almost the last thing he achieves. Hence the eccentricity and the paradox, the malice and the wantonness of the iconoclast.

The fear of losing one's job, the necessity of being somebody in a crowded and clamorous world, the terror that old age will not be secured, that your children will lack opportunity—there are a thousand terrors which arise out of the unorganized and unstable economic system under which we live. These are not terrors which can be blown away by criticism; they will go only when society is intelligent enough to have made destitution impossible, when it secures opportunity to every child, when it establishes for every human being a minimum of comfort below which he cannot sink. Then a great amount of social hesitancy will disappear. Every issue will not be fought as if life depended upon it, and mankind will have emerged from a fear economy. There are those who cannot conceive of a nation not driven by fear. They seem to feel that enterprise would diminish in a sort of placid contentment. That, it seems to me, is a serious error. The regime of fear produces dreaming and servile races, as in India and China and parts of Ireland. The enterprise that will be fruitful to modern civilization is not the undernourished child of hard necessity, but the high spirits and exuberant well-being of a happy people.

It is a common observation that no man can live well who fears death. The overcareful person is really dying all his life. He is a miser, and he pays the miser's penalty: he never enjoys his own treasure because he will not spend it. And so when we hear that he who would find his own soul must lose it first, we are not listening to an idle paradox or to some counsel of perfection. Those who hold life lightly are the real masters of it: the lavish givers have the most to give.

But anyone who picks his way through the world as if he were walking on eggs will find it a difficult and unsatisfactory place. Writers and scientists and statesmen who are forever preoccupied with their immediate reputation, always counting the costs, are buy-ing rubbish for a fortune. The thinker who has a mortal fear of being wrong will give all that is valuable in himself to that little ambition. A mistake matters far less than most of us imagine: the world is not brittle, but elastic.

If we could know the inner history of weakness, of what disap-points us in leaders, the timidity of thought, the hesitancy and the drift, we should find in endless cases that the imagination had been blinded and the will scattered by the haunting horror of constructed evils. We falter from childhood amidst shames and fears, we move in closed spaces where stale tradition enervates, we grow hysterical over success and failure, and so by surrounding instinct with terror, we prepare the soul for weakness.

There is a brilliant statement of Freud's that in the Middle Ages people withdrew to a monastery, whereas in modern times they be-come nervous. He means that formerly men could find refuge from their sense of sin, their bogeys, and their conflicts, in a special en-vironment and a fulfilling religion. But to-day they are the victims of their weakness. So if confidence is to become adequate for us we must set about expunging that weakness and disciplining a new strength.

A great deal can be done by exorcising bogeys—by refusing to add the terrors of the imagination to the terrors of fact. But there is in addition more positive work to do. We have to build up a disciplined love of the real world. It is no easy task. As yet, we see only in the vaguest way the affirmative direction of democratic cul-ture. For the breakdown of absolutism is more evident than the way to mastery.

13

Poverty, Chastity, Obedience

Poverty, chastity, and obedience are not the ideals of a self-governing people. Occasionally, however, some well-fed old gentleman announces that it would be wrong to abolish want because poverty is such an excellent training ground for character. The sentiment does not attract the poor, of course, and even the friends of the old gentleman wish that he had not made an ass of himself. And of course, there are not many modern people who could agree with the mediæval theory that celibacy is more blessed than marriage. They prefer a father and a mother to a monk and a nun, and St. Paul's dictum that it is better to marry than burn will not seem to them a very noble tribute to the family. As to obedience, they continue to like it pretty well in other people, no doubt, and yet their greatest admiration goes out to those who stand on their own feet.

These mediæval vows are the true discipline of authority. In their absolute form they were meant only for those who sought absolute perfection. But to ordinary mortals, who could accept them only in moderation, they were still the best atmosphere for a world in which democracy was impossible. I do not mean to imply that the Church deliberately created an ideal which sapped the possibility of self-government. That would be to endow the Church with an inconceivably deliberate intelligence. All I mean is that in the undemocratic world which the Church dominated, ideals grew up which expressed the truth about that world.

The desire for self-government has become vivid with the

accumulation of a great surplus of wealth. Man to-day has at last seen the possibility of freeing himself from his supreme difficulty. It wasn't easy to think much of the possibilities of this world while he lived on the edge of starvation. Resignation to hardship was a much more natural outlook. But in the midst of plenty, the imagination becomes ambitious, rebellion against misery is at last justified, and dreams have a basis in fact.

Of course, there are immense sections of the globe where the hard conditions of the older life still prevail, and there the ideal of democracy is still a very ineffective phrase. But the United States has for the most part lifted itself out of primitive hardship, and that fact, more than our supposedly democratic constitution, is what has justified in some measure the hope which inspires our history. We have been far from wise with the great treasure we possessed, and no nation has such cause for shame at the existence of poverty. We have only our short-sighted selves to blame. But the blunders are not fatal: American wealth has hardly been tapped. And that is why America still offers the greatest promise to democracy.

The first item in the program of self-government is to drag the whole population well above the misery line. To create a minimum standard of life below which no human being can fall is the most elementary duty of the democratic state. For those who go below the line of civilized decency not only suffer wretchedly: they breed the poisons of self-government. They form the famous slum proletariat about whom even the socialists despair. Occasionally some dramatic figure rises out of them, occasionally they mutter and rebel and send the newspapers into a panic. But for the purposes of constructive revolution this submerged mass is of little use, for it is harassed, beaten, helpless. These last will not be first. They may scare the rest of us into a little reform. But out of sheer wretchedness will come little of the material or the power of democracy, for as Walter Weyl [1] has said, "A man or a class, crushed to earth—is crushed to earth."

Unfit for self-government, they are the most easily led, the most easily fooled, and the most easily corrupted. You can't build a modern nation out of Georgia crackers, poverty-stricken negroes,

[1] The progressive theorist, Walter Weyl, was the author of *The New Democracy* (New York: The Macmillan Company, 1912).

the homeless and helpless of the great cities. They make a governing class essential. They are used by the forces of reaction. Once in a while they are used by revolutionists for agitation, but always they are used. Before you can begin to have democracy you need a country in which everyone has some stake and some taste of its promise.

Now to link chastity with poverty as one of the props of absolutism is to prepare for yourself a peck of trouble. "Do you advocate unchastity?" shrieks the frightened person. As unchastity means to most people promiscuity, I say emphatically, "No, it isn't unchastity that we wish." We don't wish poverty, but that doesn't mean that we are for parvenus and millionaires. And so for sex, we don't seek Don Juans or ascetics, we seek fathers and mothers, and a life that isn't swamped by sex.

Life can be swamped by sex very easily if sex is not normally satisfied. Those who can't have a piece of flesh, said Nietzsche, often grasp at a piece of spirit. I must confess I never saw anything very noble or pure in the dreams of St. Theresa. And as for St. Anthony in the Wilderness—surely that was no solution of the sex problem. But it was a wonderful way of cementing loyalty, to deny men and women a human life, and suggest that they marry the Church. The mediæval vow of chastity did not mean a sudden disappearance of the sexual life: it meant a concentration of that life upon the spiritual authority.

With poverty and chastity effectively enforced, there would have been very little need to preach obedience. That was necessary only because human nature didn't permit of any thoroughgoing application of the first two vows. Had the Church achieved its full ambition, to be glorious and rich amidst poverty, to offer the only spiritual compensation to thwarted lives, then the Church would have had few disloyal sons. But as it didn't succeed completely, it had to demand the third vow—obedience—as a kind of extra prop if the other two failed.

It is no wonder then, that the upholders of authority recognize in the labor movement and the women's awakening their mortal foes, or that Ibsen in that classic prophecy of his, should have seen in these same movements the two greatest forces for human emancipation. They are the power through which there will be accomplished that transvaluation of values which democracy means. They are pointed toward a frank worldliness, a coöperation among free people, they are pointed away from submissive want, balked impulse, and unquestioned obedience.

We can begin to see, then, a little of what democratic culture implies. There was a time, not so long ago, when scholars, and "cultured people" generally, regarded Ruskin's interest in political economy as the unfortunate perversion of a man who was born to better things. We do no longer regard it as "sordid" to take an interest in economic problems. I have met artists who deplore Mr. George Russell's interest in agricultural coöperation as unworthy of the poet who is known to the world by the mystic letters Æ. The interest of the working-class in its bread and butter problem is still occasionally the chance for a scolding about its "materialism." But in the main, modern democrats recognize that the abolition of poverty is the most immediate question before the world to-day, and they have imagination enough to know that the success of the war against poverty will be the conquest of new territory for civilized life.

So too, the day is passing when the child is taught to regard the body as a filthy thing. We train quite frankly for parenthood, not for the ecstasies of the celibate. Our interest in sex is no longer to annihilate it, but to educate it, to find civilized opportunities for its expression. We hope to organize industry and housekeeping so that normal mating shall not be a monstrously difficult problem. And there is an increasing number of people who judge sexual conduct by its results in the quality of human life. They don't think that marriage justifies licentiousness, nor will they say that every unconventional union is necessarily evil. They know the tyrannies that indissoluble marriage produces, and they are beginning to know the equal oppressions of what is called "Free love." They are becoming concrete and realistic about sex. They are saying that where love exists with self-respect and joy, where a fine environment is provided for the child, where the parents live under conditions that neither stunt the imagination nor let it run to uncontrolled fantasy, there you have the family that modern men are seeking to create. They desire such a family not because they are afraid not to advocate it, but because they have reason to believe that this is the most fruitful way of ordering human life.

When we speak of the modern intellect we mean this habit of judging rules by their results instead of by their sources. The fact that an idea is old or that it is "advanced," that the Pope said it or Bernard Shaw, all that is of no decisive importance. The real question always turns on what an idea is worth in the satisfaction of human desire.

Objections will arise at once. It will be said that you can't judge rules of life or beliefs by their results, because many an idea of the greatest value may at first be very disagreeable. In other words, it is often necessary to sacrifice immediate advantages to distant results. That is perfectly true, of course, and the balancing of present wants against the future is really the central problem of ethics. Will you weigh action by its results on this particular venture, or on your whole life, or by its results on your generation, or on the generations to come? There is no simple answer to those questions. Every human being makes his own particular compromise. There are few people so concentrated on the immediate that they don't look ahead a little, if it's only to the extent of taking out a life insurance policy. There have been a few fanatics who lived so absolutely for the millennium that they made a little hell for their companions. But the wiser a man is, it seems to me, the more vividly he can see the future as part of the evolving present. He doesn't break the flow of life, he directs it, hastens it, but preserves its continuity. The people who really matter in social affairs are neither those who wish to stop short like a mule, or leap from crag to crag like a mountain goat.

But of course, to act for results instead of in response to authority requires a readiness of thought that no one can achieve at all times. You cannot question everything radically at every moment. You have to do an infinite number of acts without thinking about their results. I have to follow the orders of my physician. We all of us have to follow the lead of specialists.

And so, it is easy to score points against anyone who suggests that modern thought is substituting the pragmatic test by results for the old obedience to authority. It can't do that altogether. We cannot be absolute pragmatists. But we judge by results as much as we can, as much as our human limitations allow. Where we have to accept dogmas without question we do so not because we have any special awe of them, but because we know that we are too ignorant, or too busy, to analyze them through. I know how un-philosophical this will sound to those who worship neatness in thought.

Well, if they can find some surer key to the complexity of life, all power to them. But let them be careful that they are not build-ing a theory which is symmetrical only on the printed page. Noth-ing is easier than to simplify life and then make a philosophy about it. The trouble is that the resulting philosophy is true only of that simplified life. If somebody can create an absolute system of beliefs and rules of conduct that will guide a business man at eleven o'clock in the morning, a boy trying to select a career, a woman in an unhappy love affair,—well then, surely no pragmatist will object. He insists only that philosophy shall come down to earth and be tried out there.

In some such spirit as I have tried to suggest, the modern world is reversing the old virtues of authority. They aimed deliberately to make men unworldly. They did not aim to found society on a full use of the earth's resources; they did not aim to use the whole nature of man; they did not intend him to think out the full expres-sion of his desires. Democracy is a turning upon those ideals in a pursuit, at first unconsciously, of the richest life that men can devise for themselves.

14

Mastery

The Dyaks of Borneo, it is said, were not accustomed to chopping down a tree, as white men do, by notching out V-shaped cuts. "Hence," says Mr. Marett[1] in telling the story, "any Dyak caught imitating the European fashion was punished by a fine. And yet so well aware were they that this method was an improvement on their own that, when they could trust each other not to tell, they would surreptitiously use it."

If you went to an elder of the Dyak race and asked him why the newer method was forbidden, he would probably have told you that it was wrong. The answer would not have satisfied you, but the Dyak would have inquired no further. What was wrong was filled with impending calamity. Now, of course, there is no end of conservatism today which is just as instinctive, just as fearful of unimagined evil, and just as dumbly irrational as the Dyaks'. I have heard a middle-aged woman say "It isn't done" as if the voice of the universe spoke through her. But there is a rationalized conservatism. If you go to an elder of the Boston race and ask why new projects are so unexceptionally bad, he will tell you that without reverence for tradition life becomes unsettled, and a nation loses itself for lack of cohesion.

These essays are based upon that observation, but added to it is the observation, just as important, that tradition will not work in the complexity of modern life. For if you ask Americans to remain true to the traditions of all their Fathers, there would

[1] The British anthropologist, Robert Ranulph Marett.

be a pretty confusion if they followed your advice. There is great confusion, as it is, due in large measure to the persistency with which men follow tradition in a world unsuited to it. They modify a bit, however, they apply "the rule of reason" to their old loyalties, and so a little adjustment is possible. But there can be no real cohesion for America in following scrupulously the inherited ideals of our people. Between the Sons of the Revolution, the Ancient Order of Hibernians, the Orangemen, the plantation life of the South, the refugees from Russia, the Balkan Slavs, there is in their traditions a conflict of prejudice and custom that would make all America as clamorous as the Stock Exchange on a busy day. Nor is there going to be lasting inspiration for Bulgarian immigrants in the legend of the Mayflower.

The only possible cohesion now is a loyalty that looks forward. America is preëminently the country where there is practical substance in Nietzsche's advice that we should live not for our fatherland but for our children's land.

To do this men have to substitute purpose for tradition: and that is, I believe, the profoundest change that has ever taken place in human history. We can no longer treat life as something that has trickled down to us. We have to deal with it deliberately, devise its social organization, alter its tools, formulate its method, educate and control it. In endless ways we put intention where custom has reigned. We break up routines, make decisions, choose our ends, select means.

The massive part of man's life has always been, and still is, subconscious. The influence of his intelligence seems insignificant in comparison with attachments and desires, brute forces, and natural catastrophes. Our life is managed from behind the scenes: we are actors in dramas that we cannot interpret. Of almost no decisive event can we say: this was our own choosing. We happen upon careers, necessity pushing, blind inclination pulling. If we stop to think we are amazed that we should be what we are. And so we have come to call mysterious everything that counts, and the more mysterious the better some of us pretend to think it is. We drift into our work, we fall in love, and our lives seem like the intermittent flicker of an obstinate lamp. War panics, and financial panics, revivals, fads sweep us before them. Men go to war not knowing why, hurl themselves at cannon as if they were bags of flour, seek impossible goals, submit to senseless wrongs, for mankind lives to-day only in the intervals of a fitful sleep.

There is indeed a dreaming quality in life: moved as it is from within by unconscious desires and habits, and from without by the brute forces of climate and soil and wind and tide. There are stretches in every day when we have no sense of ourselves at all, and men often wake up with a start: "Have I lived as long as I'm supposed to have lived? . . . Here I am, this kind of person who has passed through these experiences—well, I didn't quite know it."

That, I think, is the beginning of what we call reflection: a desire to realize the drama in which we are acting, to be awake during our own lifetime. When we cultivate reflection by watching ourselves and the world outside, the thing we call science begins. We draw the hidden into the light of consciousness, record it, compare phases of it, note its history, experiment, reflect on error, and we find that our conscious life is no longer a trivial iridescence, but a progressively powerful way of domesticating the brute.

This is what mastery means: the substitution of conscious intention for unconscious striving. Civilization, it seems to me, is just this constant effort to introduce plan where there has been clash, and purpose into the jungles of disordered growth. But to shape the world nearer to the heart's desire requires a knowledge of the heart's desire and of the world. You cannot throw yourself blindly against unknown facts and trust to luck that the result will be satisfactory.

Yet from the way many business men, minor artists, and modern philosophers talk you would think that the best world can be created by the mere conflict of economic egotisms, the mere eruption of fantasy, and the mere surge of blind instinct. There is to-day a widespread attempt to show the futility of ideas. Now in so far as this movement represents a critical insight into the emotional basis of ideas, it is a fundamental contribution to human power. But when it seeks to fall back upon the unconscious, when the return to nature is the ideal of a deliberate vegetable, this movement is like the effort of the animal that tried to eat itself: the tail could be managed and the hind legs, but the head was an insurmountable difficulty. You can have misleading ideas, but you cannot escape ideas. To give up theory, to cease formulating your desire is not to reach back, as some people imagine, to profounder sources of inspiration. It is to put yourself at the mercy of stray ideas, of ancient impositions or trumped-up fads. Accident becomes the master, the accident largely of your own training, and you become the plaything of whatever happens to have accumulated at the bottom of your mind, or to find itself sanctified in the newspaper you read and the suburb that suited your income.

There have been fine things produced in the world without intention. Most of our happiness has come to us, I imagine, by the fortunate meeting of events. But happiness has always been a precarious incident, elusive and shifting in an unaccountable world. In love, especially, men rejoice and suffer through what are to them mysterious ways. Yet when it is suggested that the intelligence must invade our unconscious life, men shrink from it as from dangerous and clumsy meddling. It is dangerous and clumsy now, but it is the path we shall have to follow. We have to penetrate the dreaming brute in ourselves, and make him answerable to our waking life.

It is a long and difficult process, one for which we are just beginning to find a method. But there is no other way that offers any hope. To shove our impulses underground by the taboo is to force them to virulent and uncontrolled expression. To follow impulse wherever it leads means the satisfaction of one impulse at the expense of all the others. The glutton and the rake can satisfy only their gluttonous and rakish impulses, and that isn't enough for happiness. What civilized men aim at is neither whim nor taboo, but a frank recognition of desire, disciplined by a knowledge of what is possible, and ordered by the conscious purpose of their lives.

There is a story that experimental psychology grew from the discovery that two astronomers trying to time the movement of the same heavenly body reached different results. It became necessary then to time the astronomers themselves in order to discount the differences in the speed of their reactions. Now whether the story is literally true or not, it is very significant. For it symbolizes the essential quality of modern science—its growing self-consciousness. There have been scientific discoveries all through the ages. Heron of

Alexandria invented a steam-turbine about 200 B.C. They had gunpowder in Ancient China. But these discoveries lay dormant, and they appear to us now as interesting accidents. What we have learned is to organize invention deliberately, to create a record for it and preserve its continuity, to subsidize it, and surround it with criticism. We have not only scientific work, but a philosophy of science, and that philosophy is the source of fruitful scientific work. We have become conscious about scientific method; we have set about studying the minds of scientists. This gives us an infinitely greater control of human invention, for we are learning to control the inventor. We are able already to discount some of the limitations of those engaged in research: we should not, for example, send a man who was color blind to report on the protective coloring of animals; we begin to see how much it matters in many investigations whether the student is an auditory or a visualizing type. Well, psychology opens up greater possibilities than this for the conscious control of scientific progress. It has begun to penetrate emotional prejudice, to show why some men are so deeply attached to authority, why philosophers have such unphilosophical likes and dislikes. We ask now of an economist, who his friends are, what his ambitions, his class bias. When one thinker exalts absolute freedom, another violent repression, we have ceased to take such ideas at their face value, and modern psychology, especially the school of Freud, has begun to work out a technique for cutting under the surface of our thoughts.

The power of criticizing the scientific mind is, I believe, our best guarantee for the progress of scientific discovery. This is the inner sanctuary of civilized power. For when science becomes its own critic it assures its own future. It is able, then, to attack the source of error itself; to forestall its own timidities, and control its own bias.

If the scientific temper were as much a part of us as the faltering ethics we now absorb in our childhood, then we might hope to face our problems with something like assurance. A mere emotion of futurity, that sense of "vital urge" which is so common to-day, will fritter itself away unless it comes under the scientific discipline, where men use language accurately, know fact from fancy, search out their own prejudice, are willing to learn from failures, and do not shrink from the long process of close observation. Then only shall we have a substitute for authority. Rightly understood science is the culture under which people can live forward in the midst of complexity, and treat life not as something given but as something to be shaped. Custom and authority will work in a simple and unchanging civilization, but in our world only those will conquer who can understand.

There is nothing accidental then in the fact that democracy in politics is the twin-brother of scientific thinking. They had to come together. As absolutism falls, science arises. It *is* self-government. For when the impulse which overthrows kings and priests and unquestioned creeds becomes self-conscious we call it science.

Inventions and laboratories, Greek words, mathematical formulæ, fat books, are only the outward sign of an attitude toward life, an attitude which is self-governing, and most adequately named humanistic. Science is the irreconcilable foe of bogeys, and therefore, a method of laying the conflicts of the soul. It is the unfrightened, masterful and humble approach to reality—the needs of our natures and the possibilities of the world. The scientific spirit is the discipline of democracy, the escape from drift, the outlook of a free man. Its direction is to distinguish fact from fancy; its "enthusiasm is for the possible"; its promise is the shaping of fact to a chastened and honest dream.

15

Modern Communion

But, you will say, granted that the breakdown of authority in a complicated world has left men spiritually homeless, and made their souls uneasy; granted that it may be possible to exorcise many of the bogeys which haunt them, and to cultivate a natural worldliness in which economic and sexual terror will have been reduced; granted that women are tending to create a new environment for the child in which the property sense will not be stimulated morbidly, and where coöperation will become as obvious as obedience and isolation were in the past; suppose too, that an expanding civilization gives such varied resources that man will live more fully, and rely less on the compensations of thwarted desire; suppose that the spirit of science pervades his daily work, not as a mutilated specialty, but as a rich interest in the world with a vivid desire to shape it,—suppose all that, would there not be lacking the one supreme virtue of the older creeds, their capacity for binding the world together?

There would be justice in such a criticism. There is a terrible loneliness that comes to men when they realize their feebleness before a brutally uninterested universe. In his own life-work, say as a teacher, a person may be making some one class-room more serviceable to a few children. But he will feel, as the more imaginative teachers do, that his work is like that of Sisyphus, he no sooner achieves a thing than it is undone. How can he educate a child for a few hours a day, when the home, the streets, the newspapers, the movies, the shop, are all busy miseducating? Wherever there is a constructive man at work you are likely to find this same complaint, that he is working alone. He may be heartwhole and eager, without bogeys or unnecessary fears. He may be free of the weaknesses that have reared so many faiths, and yet he seeks assurance in a communion with something outside himself, at the most perhaps, in a common purpose, at least, in a fellowship effort.

Religions have placed human action in a large and friendly setting. They have enabled men to play their little rôle by making it essential to the drama of eternity. "God needs me, Christ died for me, after all I may be a poor creature, but I'm indispensable." And, as if by feeling themselves part of greatness, men have added to their stature. So even the meekest freshman in a grandstand is a more exalted person because his college team has captured the front page of the newspapers. He may be merely one in thousands who cheered for the eleven heroes, yet somehow he has partaken of their heroism. He is like the cockney who talks of "our Empire," like the Irish immigrants who tell how we licked the British at Yorktown, like the crank whose society of eight people is entitled "Association for Advancing the Human Race." It is well known that in a strike it matters enormously whether the men are fighting for a "fair day's wage" or for "the emancipation of labor."

The history of martyrs is the history of people who expanded to their faith. Indeed, men have shaken destiny because they felt they embodied it. Patriotism, the Cause, Humanity, Perfection, Righteousness, Liberty,—all of them large and windy abstractions to outsiders, are more powerful than dynamite to those who feel them. "My country is the world," said Garrison, while Boston hated him. "I fight for women," says Mrs. Pankhurst. "I am a fate," said Nietzsche. "This is the true joy in life," says Bernard Shaw, "the being used for a purpose recognized by yourself as a mighty one."

It is no idle question then to ask what there is in the outlook of a modern man to bind his world together. Well, if he is looking for absolute assurance, an infallible refuge in weakness and terror, we have to answer that there is no such certainty. He may learn that while there is no promise of ultimate salvation, there is at least no fear of ultimate damnation; that in the modern world things are not so irremediable, and he may meet a large charity in its endless variety. He can find some understanding, an assurance perhaps of life's resiliency, he may come to know that nothing is so final as he thought it was, that the future is not staked on one enterprise, that life rises out of its own ashes, and renews its own opportunities. But if he demands personal guarantees, he may have to lie in order to get them.

Almost all men do require something to focus their interest in order to sustain it. A great idea like Socialism has done that for millions. But Socialism simply as a great passion can easily produce its superstitions and its barbarisms. What men need in their specialties in order to enable them to coöperate is not alone a binding passion, but a common discipline. Science, I believe, implies such a discipline. It is the fact that scientists approach the world with an understood method that enables them to give and take from each other whether they live in Calcutta or in San Francisco. The scientific world is the best example we have to-day of how specialists can coöperate. Of course there are profound disagreements, intrigues, racial and national prejudices, even among scientific men, for a common method will not wipe out the older cleavages, and it is not a perfectly cohesive force. But for the kind of civilization we are entering it is as yet the best we know.

There are undoubtedly beginnings of such a common method in public affairs. We read English books for help in dealing with American conditions. Social legislation is to-day a world-wide interest, so that reformers in Oregon may draw upon Australasian experiment.[1] The labor movement has international organization with the result that its experience becomes available for use. There is no need to multiply examples. Instruments of a coöperative mind are being forged, be it the world-wide moving picture or some immense generalization of natural science.

This work has aroused in many men the old sense of cosmic wonder, and called forth devotion to impersonal ends. Nor can it be denied that in the study of institutions, in laboratories of research, there have appeared the same loyalty and courage to which

[1] Oregon was the state in which "direct legislation" was most enthusiastically adopted. Oregon and other states drew on Australia's development of the secret or "Australian" ballot. New Zealand early adopted the referendum, taxation of land monopoly, and various kinds of public ownership.

the old religions could point as to their finest flower. Moreover, these devotions which science can show, come in the main redeemed from barbarism and pointed to civilized use. There is, to be sure, a certain raw novelty in modern forms of devotion, as there is in uninhabited houses, in new clothes and in new wine—they have hardly felt the mellowing of human contact, that saturation of brute things with the qualities of their users, which makes men love the old, the inadequate, the foolish, as against what is sane and clean, but unfamiliar. Science, too, is a concrete and essentially humble enterprise; spiritually sufficient it may be, to-day, only for the more robust. But the release from economic want, the emancipation from manufactured bogeys, the franker acceptance of normal desire, should tend to make men surer of themselves. And so most of them may not find it necessary to believe the impossible, but will reach their satisfaction in contemplating reality, in decorating it, shaping it, and conquering it.

They may find, as Santayana suggests, that "to see better what we now see, to see by anticipation what we should actually see under other conditions, is wonderfully to satisfy curiosity and to enlighten conduct. At the same time, scientific thinking involves no less inward excitement than dramatic fiction does. It summons before us an even larger number of objects in their fatal direction upon our interests. Were science adequate it would indeed absorb those passions which now, since they must be satisfied somehow, have to be satisfied by dramatic myths. . . . All pertinent dramatic emotion, joyous or tragic, would then inhere in practical knowledge. As it is, however, science abstracts from the more musical overtones of things in order to trace the gross and basal processes within them; so that the pursuit of science seems comparatively dry and laborious, except where at moments the vista opens through to the ultimate or leads back to the immediate. Then, perhaps, we recognize that in science we are surveying all it concerns us to know, and in so doing are becoming all that it profits us to be."

For the discipline of science is the only one which gives any assurance that from the same set of facts men will come approximately to the same conclusion. And as the modern world can be civilized only by the effort of innumerable people we have a right to call science the discipline of democracy. No omnipotent ruler can deal with our world, nor the scattered anarchy of individual temperaments. Mastery is inevitably a matter of coöperation, which means that a great variety of people working in different ways must find some order in their specialties. They will find it, I think, in a common discipline which distinguishes between fact and fancy, and works always with the implied resolution to make the best out of what is possible.

For behind this development of common method there are profound desires at work. As yet they are vaguely humanitarian. But they can be enriched by withdrawing them from vague fantasy in order to center them on a conception of what human life might be. This is what morality meant to the Greeks in their best period, an estimate of what was valuable, not a code of what should be forbidden. It is this task that morality must resume, for with the reappearance of a deliberate worldliness, it means again a searching for the sources of earthly happiness.

In some men this quest may lead to luminous passion. "The state-making dream," Wells calls it, and he speaks of those who "have imagined cities grown more powerful and peoples made rich and multitudinous by their efforts, they thought in terms of harbors and shining navies, great roads engineered marvellously, jungles cleared and deserts conquered, the ending of muddle and dirt and misery; the ending of confusions that waste human possibilities; they thought of these things with passion and desire as other men think of the soft lines and tender beauty of women. Thousands of men there are to-day almost mastered by this white passion of statecraft, and in nearly everyone who reads and thinks you could find, I suspect, some sort of answering response." And then with careful truth he adds, "But in every one it presents itself extraordinarily entangled and mixed up with other, more intimate things."

We begin to recognize a vague spirit which may suggest a common purpose. We live in a fellowship with scientists whose books we cannot read, with educators whose work we do not understand. Conservative critics laugh at what they call the futurist habit of mind. It is very easy to point out how blind and unintelligent is the enthusiasm of liberal people, how eager they are to accept Bergson, Montessori, Freud and the Cubists. But there is something fundamentally dull in these sneers. For granted the faddishness of modern people, there is yet more than faddishness in being friendly to novelty in a novel environment. It is the glimmer of intention, the absurd, human contradictory sign of faith. Men call it by different names—progress, the welfare of the race—it is perhaps not ready for precise formulation in a neat and inspiring slogan. But nevertheless, it is the business of critics to understand these beginnings, for they are already a great practical force. They enable men to share their hopes with strangers, to travel about and talk to people of widely different professions and origin, yet to find the assurance that they are part of a great undertaking.

16

Fact and Fancy

Most people still feel that there is something inhuman about the scientific attitude. They think at once of a world grown over-precise, of love regulated by galvanometers and sphygmographs, of table talk abolished because nutrition is confined to capsules prepared in a laboratory, of babies brought up in incubators. Instead of desire, statistical abstracts; a chilly, measured, weighed, and labelled existence. There is a famous cartoon of Max Beerbohm's in which H. G. Wells is depicted "conjuring up the darling future." A spectacled mother holds in her arm a spectacled infant, mostly head like a pollywog, while she dangles before it a pair of geometrical dividers. Mr. Chesterton's nightmare of a future in which jolly beer and jolly dirt and jolly superstition shall have disappeared is merely a somewhat violently literary expression of what the average man feels. Science as it comes through the newspapers announces that kissing is unhygienic and that love is a form of lunacy. Science is the occupation of absent-minded professors, of difficult and unsociable persons, wise enough, no doubt, but not altogether in their right minds. And then, of course, when wireless telegraphy is perfected, science becomes an omnipotent magic, wonderful or fearful, infinite in its power, but always something above and beyond the ordinary thoughts of men. So the suggestion that Twentieth Century democracy is bound up with the progress of the scientific spirit will make many people think of

Organized charity, all cold and iced,
In the name of a cautious, statistical Christ.

There is a basis for these fears. Scientists have often been very arrogant, unnecessarily sure of themselves, and only too glad to pooh-pooh what they couldn't fit into some theory. This was especially true of those who grew up in the controversies of the nineteenth century. There was a kind of malicious fun in telling a devout man that thought depended on phosphor and that his magnificent visions were merely an excitation of the cortex. Of course, far-seeing men like Huxley protested that the sensation of red had not been destroyed because light-waves had been measured.

Yet there were plenty of scientific bigots who would have liked to annihilate what they could not weigh. Certainly it is true that the general effect of science at first was to create impatience with the emotional life. Many proud possessors of the Spencerian mind devoted their glowing youth to a study of those bleak books which used to pass for scientific manuals. They regarded religion with scorn and art with condescension, and sometimes they nerved themselves up to admire beauty as one of the necessary weaknesses of an otherwise reasonable man. Truth for them was as neat as a checkerboard, and they made you feel like the man from Corinth who asked a Spartan "whether the trees grew square in his country."

It always surprises one of these hard-headed people to be told that he lives in a world, which has a fantastic resemblance to a cubist painting. For the rationalist's vision expresses his own love of form, while it distorts the object. Now in a thinker who pretends to be dealing with actual events this is a dangerous delusion. He will come to believe that square things, sharply defined things, very tangible things, are somehow more genuine than elusive and changing ones. It's a short step from this to denying the existence of anything which is not easily defined. But note what he has done: seduced by a method of thought, the rigorous, classifying method where each color is all one tone, he has come to regard his method as more important than the blendings and interweavings of reality. Like any dreamer he gives up the search for truth in order to coddle himself in his simple, private universe. The hardness of such a rationalist is on the surface only: at bottom there is a weakness which clings to stiff and solid frames of thought because the subtlety of life is distressing.

It is a great deal easier, for example, to talk of Labor and Capital than to keep in mind all the different kinds of workers or how they shade off into capitalists. It is immensely difficult to think about the actual complexity in the relations of men, and that is why eager and active people substitute for the facts those large abstractions with their rigid simplicity. But the workingman who is something of a capitalist himself, the employer who works as hard as anyone under him, can't see how the straight conflict between Exploited and Exploiter, Labor and Capital, applies in the particular situation.

What puzzles them is one of the oldest difficulties of thought: that any large classification fits each single fact very badly. They are like "the bewildered porter in Punch" quoted by Graham Wallas, "who had to arrange the subtleties of nature according to the unsubtle tariff-schedule of his company. 'Cats . . . is dogs, and guinea-pigs is dogs, but this 'ere tortoise is a hinsect.' "

Now we all have to do the same injustice to the tortoise, or in the language of philosophy, we have to use concepts. How much we shall use them depends upon what we are trying to do. For the purposes of the soap-box a few very rough distinctions are about all anyone can handle. In a group of friends, you can be a bit subtler. The moment you act in some real situation, say in some labor dispute, your large generalizations have to undergo enormous modification. For you will find yourself dealing there with a particular employer who is not exactly like any other employer and with workers for whom race and education, the fact that it's a cold winter, and a hundred other little complications turn the balance.

The only rule to follow, it seems to me, is that of James: "Use concepts when they help, and drop them when they hinder understanding." For "the world we practically live in is one in which it is impossible, except by theoretic retrospection, to disentangle the contributions of intellect from those of sense. They are wrapped and rolled together as a gunshot in the mountains is wrapt and rolled in fold on fold of echo and reverberative clamor. . . . The two mental functions thus play into each other's hands. Perception prompts our thought, and thought in turn enriches our perception. The more we see, the more we think; while the more we think, the more we see in our immediate experiences, and the greater grows the detail and the more significant the articulateness of our perception."

There is nothing in the scientific temper which need make it inevitably hostile to the variety of life. But many scientists have been hostile. And the reason for that is not so difficult to see. The first triumphs of the scientific mind were in mathematics, astronomy, and physics, out of which grows engineering. The habit of mind which produced such great results was naturally exalted, so that men began to feel that science which wasn't mechanical, wasn't science. They dreamt of a time when living bodies, consciousness and human relations, would be adjusted with the accuracy of a machine. But they were merely following an analogy, which a real scientist would abandon the moment it appeared that living organisms differ from the inert. I do not know whether any such distinction must be made, but there is nothing in the scientific temper which would preclude it.

In the long controversy with religious belief the true temper of the scientific mind was revealed. There have been hasty people who announcd boldly that any interest in the immortality of the soul was "unscientific." William James, in fact, was accused of treason because he listened to mystics and indulged in psychical research. Wasn't he opening the gates to superstition and obscurantism? It was an ignorant attack. For the attitude of William James toward "ghosts" was the very opposite of blind belief. He listened to evidence. No apostle of authority can find the least comfort in that. For the moment you test belief by experience you have destroyed the whole structure of authority. It may well happen that the growth of knowledge will prove the wisdom in many a popular saying, or confirm the truth of a "superstition." It would be surprising if it didn't, for the long adjustments of the race must have accumulated much unconscious truth. But when these truths are held because there is evidence for them, their whole character is changed. They are no longer blind beliefs; they are subject to amendment when new evidence appears, and their danger is gone.

The last few years have produced a striking illustration of this within the Catholic Church. The Modernist movement is nothing but an outburst of the scientific spirit in the very citadel of authority. For the Modernists propose to accept Catholicism on the basis of experience. It is no wonder, then, that the Pope issued his Encyclical letter denouncing the Modernists root and branch, for once you substitute evidence for authoritative revelation the ruin of absolutism is prepared. There is no compromise possible between authority and the scientific spirit. They may happen to agree on some particular point to-day, but there is no guarantee that they will not disagree to-morrow. The Modernist may subscribe to the whole creed, but from the point of view of the absolutist his heresy is of the deepest and subtlest kind. All the fixity of eternal principles comes crashing about your head if you derive them simply from human experience. There is a sentence of Santayana's which destroys with a terrible brevity the ambitions of those who accept the scientific spirit and cling to traditional authority. "The gods are demonstrable only as hypotheses but as hypotheses they are not gods."

There is no question that science has won its way, in part, by insult and blindness, often by a harsh ignorance of the value of older creeds. It is associated with a certain hardness of mind and narrowness of feeling, as if it were a vandal in a sanctuary. But that also is not essential to the scientific mind; it is rather an accompaniment of the bitter controversy in which science grew up.

We can begin now to define the attitude of science toward the past. It may be summed up, I think, by saying that only when we have destroyed the authority of tradition can we appreciate its treasure. So long as tradition is a blind command it is for our world an evil and dangerous thing. But once you see the past merely as a theater of human effort, it overflows with suggestion.

Men can reverence the dead if they are buried. But they will no longer sit at table with corpses, ghosts, and skeletons. They can respect both life and death; they must resent a confusion of life and death. The conservative has made such a confusion, and out of it arises our contempt for the traditionalist mind. Scorn of the antiquarian has been transferred to antiquity. Modern men have said in a way that rather than deal with the past through a conservative, they would leave it to him as his exclusive domain.

There is hardly need to rehearse the grounds of this contempt.

Whenever evil is defended or tyranny devised, it is done in the name of tradition. So the loss of a sense of the past has come to mean a definite emancipation. Then, too, it looks at times as if men felt they could not move forward if they stared backward,—that Greece and Rome are a fatal lure which enervate and render dry-as-dust. They think of pedants in closed university ground, walled in from all enthusiasm, tangled in the creepers that shackle with their beauty.

Modern men are afraid of the past. It is a record of human achievement, but its other face is human defeat. Too often it speaks through the words of Koheleth[1] the Preacher,—that which is crooked cannot be made straight. History is full of unbearable analogies which make enthusiasm cold and stale. It tells of the complications that are not foreseen, of the successes that caricature the vision. Conservatives may dwell upon the perspective which history gives. It is just this perspective which men fear, the looking at life through the wrong end of the opera glass. It is a good instinct which refuses to see the present as a bubble on the stream of time. For the bubble in which we live is more of our concern than all the rivers which have flowed into the sea.

And yet, the past can be a way to freedom. The present order is held very lightly and without undue reverence in a mind which knows how varied is human experience. An imagination fed on the past will come to see the present as a very temporary thing. Wherever routine and convention become unbearable weights, the abundance of the past is a source of liberty. Merely to realize that your way of living is not the only way, is to free yourself from its authority. It brings a kind of lucidity in which society is rocked by a devastating Why? Why should men who have one life to live submit to the drudgeries and vexations that we call civilization? The whole shell is strained by a wild rationality.

The past has been used to throttle the present. Why should we not turn around and use it for a different purpose? We have sunk under the weight of its gloomy sanctity. Can we not free ourselves in the light of its great variety?

That is just what the best scholarship of our time has tried to do.

---

[1] Koheleth, the Hebrew word for the Old Testament book called by the Greek word, Ecclesiastes.

The Nineteenth Century undoubtedly meant a shattering of the traditional faiths. And yet no century has ever been so eager to understand the very idols it was breaking. The same period in which the secular spirit won its greatest triumphs saw the first real effort at an understanding of superstition and magic, ritual and taboo, religious need and doctrinal sources. Indeed, the interest of the scientific spirit in the past has been so masterful that all previous history looks like village gossip. It is utterly untrue, therefore, to say that the modern outlook means an abrupt break with the accumulated wisdom of the past. It has meant a break with blind obedience to an ignorant fabrication about the past. But that break is what has opened to us the lessons of history as they have never been opened to any other people. It has been said that we know more about Homer than Plato did; no one would dream of comparing the modern knowledge of classical antiquity with Dante's or with Shakespeare's. The Biblical scholars of the last hundred years, in spite of all their so-called atheism, have, I believe, seen deeper into the basis of Christianity than the Church which has represented it. And while they have undoubtedly shaken authority, they have built up a sympathetic understanding of the human values it contained. All this is the sheerest commonplace, yet conservatives continue to accuse the scientific spirit of blindness to the great past. They deceive themselves in their outcry. They don't really fear a neglect of the past. They don't really mean that modern men ignore it. What they miss in modern science is submission. They feel vaguely that scientific interest in the past makes of history a double-edged weapon. The absolutist has suddenly discovered that a study of the very thing he adores destroys obedience to it. The men who talk most about reverence for the American Constitution are the last people in the world to welcome a study of its origin. For the conservative is not devoted to a real past. He is devoted to his own comfortable image of it.

We have come to look at history with ease and without too much reverence. To be sure that puts a bridle on a great deal of haphazard optimism. There is a strain of doubt in the speculations of an historian. But there is a full compensation for the loss of barren hopes in the bodily warmth that comes from knowing how millions of men have acted, have hoped, have built better than they knew, or failed. If the dream of perfection and endless progress fades, is that necessarily so great a loss? It does not seem possible that life will lose its flavor because we have robbed it of a few abstract and careless dreams. For the modern sense of what the past contains can give a new realization of the fertility in existence. That is a rock upon which to build. Instead of a "featureless future," instead of an aspiring vacuum, which ends in disappointment, we may see a more modest future, but one inhabited by living people. This is the great boon of the past, that it saturates thought with concrete images. And it leaves scope for invention, for the control of nature and buoyant living. For by taking with a certain levity our schemes for improvement we shatter the sects and liberate thought.

There is, however, a persistent feeling that science means the abandonment of the imagination for a grubby absorption in facts. It is far truer to say that with the scientific spirit the imagination comes into its own. Fantasy has been a solace in defeat, a refuge from reality, a compensation to the thwarted, a dreaming desire for better things. But under the discipline of science, desire becomes concrete: it not only imagines, but it creates as well. So we can say with real justice that vision is for the first time able to direct the shaping of a world.

One of the myths that modern critics are overthrowing is the notion that science is a passionless pursuit of dead facts. For even in the most "disinterested" inquiry, there is, as Bertrand Russell says, some interest that determines the direction of our curiosity. Men will endow medical schools and institutes of technology, but only very idle and superfluously rich persons would think of devoting much time to the use of adverbs in the Bible or to the comparative history of Icelandic particles. Science is a very human thing. It springs from a need, is directed by curiosity to choose an interesting field of study, and in that field seeks results that concern men. The ideal of science, it seems to me, is to seek interesting truth critical of one's interest. If the student is merely disinterested, he is a pedant; if he seeks only what catches his passing fancy, he is romantic. The true scientist is inspired by a vision without being the victim of it.

Before the scientific spirit can reach its full bloom, it will have to acquire an honest sense of the rôle that fantasy plays in all its work. This is true especially of the social sciences. We are just beginning to realize the importance in economics of the economist's utopia. We are learning the determining influence of a thinker's dream. Thus Adam Smith's utopia was a place where enterprise was unshackled: he longed for a freedom which the corporate guilds and feudal restrictions of his time denied. He had seen Watts persecuted for his steam engine; had seen him take refuge in the university grounds at Glasgow from a crusted society that had no use for disturbing inventions. So Adam Smith endowed nature and men with the virtues that Eighteenth Century England lacked,— he dreamed his utopia of laissez-faire. Guided by that utopia, he sought facts and built arguments into a science of economics. He justified his dream. It was timely, for it uttered the hopes of England. His facts were plausible almost immediately, his arguments swam with the flood-tide of opinion. The "Wealth of Nations" became the Bible of English trade,—like all Bibles it was true to hope and practical for those who used it.

One man, at least, in the Nineteenth Century, achieved a result similar to Adam Smith's. Ricardo didn't. As Prof. Marshall points out, Ricardo, who was a stockbroker, erected the "pure science" of economics on the very limited motives he knew. Even a fine spirit like John Stuart Mill was doomed to a large measure of sterility because he did not grasp the revolutionary dream that was rising in his time. What Ricardo had no idea of doing, what Mill failed to do, Karl Marx did. In his own time, the '50's and '60's, Marx saw through a bewildering maze of facts and put his hand upon the revolutionary trend. And so he stood in as commanding a position to the middle age of capitalism as Adam Smith did to its infancy. Marx won out, not because his books are easy reading: they are not, except for occasional bursts of irony and wrath. He did not win out because the respectable of the world founded universities in his honor; they didn't. He won out because his vision was a rising one in the facts of his time.

The facts have changed in sixty years, and with them our vision: Marx was not omniscient, and the revolutionary movement is no longer adequately expressed by him. You do not have to go to the hostile critics of Marx. The inadequacy of Marx for the present age is freely admitted by a rising group within the socialist movement. In many essential ways, events have not justified his prophecies. The middle class has not disappeared: in this country it is the dominant power expressing itself through the Progressives, and through the Wilson Administration. The middle class has put the "Money Power" on the defensive. Big business is losing its control of the government. The farmers are a class with enormous power, misunderstood and neglected by the city-bred theories of socialism. The great line-up of two hostile classes hasn't happened. There have been fierce conflicts between employers and employees, but a united working class facing united capitalists is an unreal picture of American conditions. Labor has within itself innumerable deep conflicts of interest. Business men are divided by trades and by sections. And there is an unexpected burst of sheerly democratic impulse which blurs class lines. Internationalism is still a very distant dream, and while men are less provincial, it is doubtful whether the national idea is any weaker. Patriotism itself has gained a new dignity by its increasing alliance with democratic reform, and there is actually ground for supposing that love of country is coming to mean love of country and not hatred of other countries. There is a growth of that abused thing, public spirit, and the growth is so powerful that it may be able to ride the mere clashing of self-interest.

I repeat these commonplaces with no intention of casting any doubts upon the historic service of Karl Marx. If they go to show anything it is this: that the probabilities have changed, and that only by expressing that fact can *our* social science be built up. Adam Smith and Karl Marx, each in his own way, took a revolutionary purpose and expressed it. One can say without fear of contradiction that they are the two most fertile minds that have dealt with the modern problem. But the orthodox economists and the orthodox Marxians are out of touch with the latent forces of this age: both have proved themselves largely sterile. They have built a dialectic, one might almost say, a dialect, upon the texts of their masters; they have lost their command over change, and so they have become apologetic, and eager to save their faces in the wreck of their creed. The effect on socialism has been very disastrous. In America, to borrow no unnecessary trouble, socialist thinking has almost come to a standstill. The leaders of the movement write one weary book after another in which the old formulæ are restated. But not a single study of any depth has been made by an American Marxian of the American trust, trade union, political system or foreign policy. And as for the underlying spiritual habits of the American people, there is hardly any recognition that such habits exist. There has been on the other hand a very noticeable hostility to original effort. Yet even if Karl Marx captured the secret of social evolution (which is doubtful), and even if Karl Kautsky is his vicar,[2] the necessity still remains of showing concretely how that key unlocks the American difficulty. A principle is at best a guide: it is certainly not an open sesame to the future to be applied without hesitation by any pamphleteer. It is no longer very illuminating to meet the American problem with the stale vision of continental Europe in 1850.

The first way to estimate a social philosophy is to test the vision which it embodies. For this is what determines the direction of the thinker's interest, and from it his arguments take their lead. But you cannot always trust his own statement as to his purpose. Every thinker is abstractedly devoted to truth, and almost everybody presents himself as a lover of justice and righteousness. But he may see justice in almost anything,—in the unfettered action of business men, or the "dictatorship of the proletariat." Real criticism would find out what he sees and admires instinctively,—what are, in short, the governing assumptions of his thought. Thus Woodrow Wilson's "New Freedom" is laid in the main upon sympathy with "those on the make," with the man looking for a career; upon horror at the crimes of monopoly, and little recognition of the crimes of competition. It is, I believe, a vigorous restatement of the traditional American utopia in which justice is to be attained by the balance of self-interest. There is a kind of hope that an equality in push will neutralize all dangers, and produce an automatic coöperation. So Wilson seems to see the working man merely as a possible shopkeeper. The assumptions are those of a generous commercialism. It is a vision of chivalrous enterprise. Or take the message of Haywood: he sees the unskilled laborer, the genuine proletarian without property in things or in craft; he sees the outcast, the

---

[2] The German Socialist Karl Kautsky headed the movement which accused the "revisionists" of compromising Marxist orthodoxy.

convict, the casual, the bum, the peon, with such wonderful warmth and great understanding that they have come to embody for him the whole social problem. What are the troubles of a business man harassed by a bad credit system to these ultimate miseries in which are concentrated the failures of our civilization? Do you think there will be any "reason" for Haywood in a social philosophy which seems to forget the very things which fill his sky? He has only to take a walk through Union Square to feel what fools his critics are.

It may seem curious to approach a pretentiously scientific volume with the question: What is this man's dearest wish? The usual method is to regard that as of no importance, and to turn immediately to testing of logic or criticism of fact. It is no wonder that writers are not convinced by hostile reviews, or that editorials make so little impression on propagandists. Unless you go to the passionate source of ideas, you are a cat looking at a king. What does it matter to the suffragettes that they are called hysterical and lectured about their mistaken tactics? That is so much scrubby, withered stupidity fit only to set off vividly the grandeur of ideas it attacks. Or does anyone suppose that feminism is dependent on the logic of its supporters or opponents? Certainly not. Until you begin to see in feminism the opposition of attitudes toward life, drawn by hope and pushed by events, you are still the six-weeks convert who can rattle off her argument and repartee in a fusillade across the dinner-table.

Criticism will have to slough off the prejudices of the older rationalism if it is to have any radical influence on ideas. It is sophomoric to suppose that the emotional life can be treated as a decadent survival. Men's desires are not something barbaric which the intellect must shun. Their desires are what make their lives, they are what move and govern. You are not talking of human beings when you talk of "pure reason." And, therefore, anyone who deepens the conflict between thought and feeling is merely adding confusion to difficulty. The practical line of construction is to saturate feeling with ideas. That is the only way in which men can tap their own power,—by passionate ideas. There is, of course, no greater difficulty in thought than to attain a delicate adjustment of our own desires to what is possible. All important thinking achieves such an adjustment, and we recognize its success by the fact that it gives us control over brute things. That sense of control is the yielding of fact to intelligent desire. But if we try to ignore the desire that moves our thought, if we try in short to be "absolutely objective," we succeed only in accumulating useless facts, or we become the unconscious victims of our wishes. If thinking didn't serve desire, it would be the most useless occupation in the world.

The only reason, of course, for casting suspicion upon the emotional life is that it does so often falsify the world and build a fool's paradise in a human hell. But when you have faced this fully, there is still no reason for attempting the vain effort of jumping out of our human skins. The danger means simply that desire has to be subjected to criticism. It is a difficult task. But it is one that we are capable of beginning, for the great triumph of modern psychology is its growing capacity for penetrating to the desires that govern our thought.

There have been a large number of very frank attempts to express the vision of an ideal commonwealth. Plato, More, Bacon, Campanella, Fourier, William Morris, Bellamy, H. G. Wells, are only a few among many. From them come the obvious utopias, pictures of a better world by gifted and dissatisfied men. They are strangely alike. Generally the utopia is located in Peru, or a mythical island, or in the year two thousand, or centuries back, or Nowhere. Life is fixed: the notion of change is rare, for men do not easily associate perfection with movement. Moreover, the citizens of these utopias are the disciplined servants of the community. They are rigorously planned types with sharply defined careers laid out for them from birth to death. A real man would regard this ideal life as an unmitigated tyranny. But why are the utopias tyrannical? I imagine it is because the dreamer's notion of perfection is a place where everything and everybody is the puppet of his will. In a happy dream the dreamer is omnipotent: that is why it is a happy dream. So utopias tend toward a scrupulous order, eating in common mess halls, mating by order of the state, working as the servant of the community. There is no democracy in a utopia,—no willingness to allow intractable human beings the pleasure of going to the devil in their own way. Even in the utopias which pretend to be democratic, that is, where the citizens vote, the assumption always exists that the citizens vote as the dreamer would have them vote. He simply calls his will the will of the people.

Now these qualities, so obvious in the utopias, can be detected in all sorts of thinking which would be horrified at the word utopian. Most economics is about life either on Robinson Crusoe's island, or at least in some imaginary and ideally simplified nation. Few economists can remember that their reasoning is built upon an unreal picture of man and industry. By the time the details are worked out, economists have the greatest difficulty in recalling the fact that they have been talking about an imaginary world, a world which pleases their fancy because it yields to their logic.

Classical economics is related to the utopias in that it deals with some place, not England and not the United States, where motives are utterly simple, and rigorously automatic. The imaginary world of the economist is not, however, a generous fantasy of a fine life. It is a crass abstraction, industrialism idealized until it is no longer industrialism.

The bureaucratic dreams of reformers often bear a striking resemblance to the honest fantasies of the utopians. What we are coming to call "State Socialism" is in fact an attempt to impose a benevolent governing class on humanity. Oh, for wise and powerful officials to bring order out of chaos, end the "muddle," and make men clean, sober and civic-minded. There is no real understanding of democracy in the State Socialist, for he doesn't attempt to build with the assent and voluntary coöperation of men and women. But he avoids the laborious and disheartening method of popular education, and takes satisfaction in devising a ruling class, inspired by him, as a short-cut to perfection.

But let no one suppose that the "revolutionist" who denounces State Socialism is thereby free from the utopian habit of mind. He may scorn the brutal fictions of the economist or the depressing benevolence of the bureaucrat, only to imagine a world more unreal than either. I have before me a syndicalist utopia written by two of the most prominent leaders in France. It is a picture of the Revolution which is going to happen. The working men of France do just what the syndicalist dream says they should do. Suddenly, when the crash comes, there is an exhibition of skill in organizing;

there rises to the surface a coöperative power epoch-making in the history of the race. Millions of men who fight and curse each other every day, their interests divided by trade and locality, suddenly become unanimous and efficient. Why? Because the authors of the book would like it so, because they have imagined that their will had become the will of the people. They have treated French working men as the puppets of their fancy.

And yet, as Oscar Wilde said, no map of the world is worth a glance that hasn't Utopia on it. Our business is not to lay aside the dream, but to make it plausible. We have to aim at visions of the possible by subjecting fancy to criticism. The usual thing to do is to follow fiction unreservedly: that produces the castle in Spain and news from nowhere. Or to deny fancy, and suppress it: that means that the thinker becomes the victim of his prejudice, the unconscious slave of his desires. The third course is to drag dreams out into the light of day, show their sources, compare them with fact, transform them to possibilities. They should not run wild. They cannot be discarded. So they must be disciplined. For modern civilization demands something greater than the fantasies of a child or the close observation of patient investigators, something greater that is born of their union: it calls for a dream that suffuses the actual with a sense of the possible.

This is the creative imagination, and to it we owe all attempts to bridge the gap between what we wish and what we have. Romanticism can falter: "it would be lovely, if——"; Philistia can answer: "what is, is"; but the disciplined imagination alone can say, "I will." Mere fantasy gives up the struggle with actual affairs in order to find a temporary home in the warmth of memory and the fervor of impossible hopes. So in the intimacies of his own life each man confesses by his dreams that he and his world are at odds: that his desires overflow experience and ask for more than they can ever have. If he remains there, he may build splendid utopias, and shirk the effort to realize them; he is the eternal Peer Gynt, hero of his own epic, dawdler and coward in the world. He is uncompromising in his dreams, and acquiescent in his deeds. At the other pole is the philistine with his smug sense of the comfort of life, pledged to his routine, convinced that change is over, satisfied that he and his are the pinnacles of creation. Nothing is possible for him, because nothing more is desirable: the long travail of creation is done, and there he is. To all wild dreams he presents a shrewd and well-seasoned knowledge of genuine affairs. Vision beats in vain against his solid world.

In the creative imagination no relevant fact is shirked; yet over all the things that are there hovers a feeling for what they might be. A sharp and clear sense of existence is shot through with the light of its possibilities. Each fact is a place where the roads fork. Each event is a vista. Each moment is a choice. To the man who lives without question from day to day, life is just one thing after another; to the mere dreamer it is harsh and unyielding. But to the creative imagination fact is plastic, and ready to be moulded by him who understands it.

That, I believe, is the spirit of invention: around each observation there gathers an aura of conjectures. The scientific discoverer can penetrate the crevices of fact with moving guesses; each experiment is suspended in pregnant hypotheses. It is the spirit of the working artist, embodied in the fine myth that the block of marble imprisoned a statue which the sculptor released. To the artist his material is not dead clay or a silent palette, but a living substance clamoring for its form. It is the dilettante who could do a fine work if it weren't for the hardness of the stone. It is the esthete who can do everything but write his poems. It is the amateur who complains about the conflict between matter and spirit. Not the producing artist: his medium is a friendly thing, the very substance of his dream. It is the spirit of education: not to produce a row of respectable automata, but to draw out of each child the promise that is in it.

It is the spirit of valuable statecraft: the genius among politicians is he who can deal in his own time with the social forces that lead to a better one. He does not ask for a world of angels before he can begin. He does not think his duty in life is merely to keep old institutions in good repair. He grasps the facts of his age, sees in the confusion of events currents like the union, the trust, the coöperative,—suffuses them with their promise, and directs them into the structure of the future.

It is the spirit of all fine living: to live ready, to lighten experience by a knowledge of its alternatives, to let no fact be opaque, but to make what happens transparent with the choices it offers. To escape from barren routine and vain fantasy in order to leaven reality with its possibilities: this must be the endless effort of a democratic people. To stand-pat on whatever happens to exist is to put yourself at the mercy of all the blind mutterings and brute forces that move beneath the surface of events. The labor movement, the women's awakening, industry on a national scale, will work themselves out to distorted and wasted ends, if they come merely as blind pushes against invincible ignorance. But if they are left to themselves, if the labor movement becomes the plaything of its own visions, if it is not welded and disciplined to the other interests of civilization, then its wonderful possibilities will be frittered away. And likewise, so long as the large organization of business is in the hands of economic adventurers or attacked by its defeated competitors, there is no chance to make of it what it could be.

The method of a self-governing people is to meet every issue with an affirmative proposal which draws its strength from some latent promise. Thus the real remedy for violence in industrial disputes is to give labor power that brings responsibility. The remedy for commercialism is collective organization in which the profiteer has given way to the industrial statesman. The incentive to efficiency is not alone love of competent work but a desire to get greater social values out of human life. The way out of corrupt and inept politics is to use the political state for interesting and important purposes. The unrest of women cannot be met by a few negative freedoms: only the finding of careers and the creation of positive functions can make liberty valuable. In the drift of our emotional life, the genuine hope is to substitute for terror and weakness, a frank and open worldliness, a love of mortal things in the discipline of science.

These are not idle dreams: they are, it seems to me, concrete possibilities of the actual world in which we live. I have tried in this book to suggest a few of them, to make clearer to myself by illustrations, the attitude of mind with which we can begin to approach our strangely complex world. It lacks precision, it lacks the definiteness of a panacea, and all of us rebel against that. But mastery in our world cannot mean any single, neat, and absolute line of procedure. There is something multitudinous about the very notion of democracy, something that offends our inherited intellectual prejudices. This book would have a more dramatic climax if I could say that mastery consisted in some one thing: say in a big union of the working class, or the nationalization of all business. But it isn't possible to say that because there are too many factors which compete for a place, too many forces that disturb a simple formula. Mastery, whether we like it or not, is an immense collaboration, in which all the promises of to-day will have their vote.

Our business as critics is to make those promises evident, to give to the men who embody them a consciousness of them, to show how they clash with facts, to bathe them in suggestion. In that atmosphere we can go about organizing the new structure of society, building up producers' and consumers' controls, laying down plans for wise uses of our natural resources, working wherever we happen to be, or wherever our abilities call us, on the substitution of design for accident, human purposes for brute destiny. It is not easy, nor as yet a normal attitude toward life. The sustained effort it requires is so great that few can maintain it for any length of time. Anyone who has tried will report that no intellectual discipline is comparable in the severity of its demands: from the weariness it engenders men fall either into sheer speculation or mechanical repetition. How often does a book begin truly, and turn off exhausted into a conventional ending. You can almost see the point where the author gave up his struggle, and called in the claptrap of a happy accident. How often does a reformer begin with penetration, entangle himself in officialdom, and end in excuses for uninspired deeds. Who has not wept over the critical paper which started off so bravely, handling each event with freshness and skill, only to become cluttered in its own successes and redundant with stale virtues. Everyone has met the man who approached life eagerly and tapered off to a middle age where the effort is over, his opinions formed, his habits immutable, with nothing to do but live in the house he has built, and sip what he has brewed.

Effort wells up, beats bravely against reality, and in weariness simmers down into routine or fantasy. No doubt much of this is due to physiological causes, some of which lie beyond our present control. And yet in large measure the explanation lies elsewhere. There are fine maturities to give our pessimism the lie. This abandonment of effort is due, I imagine, to the fact that the conscious mastery of experience is, comparatively speaking, a new turn in human culture. The old absolutisms of caste and church and state made more modest demands than democracy does: life was settled and fantasy was organized into ritual and riveted by authority. But the modern world swings wide and loose, it has thrown men upon their own responsibility. And for that gigantic task they lack experience, they are fettered and bound and finally broken by ancient terrors that huddle about them. Think of the enormous effort that goes into mere rebellion, think of the struggle that young men and women go through in what they call a fight for independence, independence which is nothing but an opportunity to begin. They have to break with habits rooted in the animal loyalties of their childhood, and the rupture has consequences greater than most people realize. The scars are very deep, even the most successful rebel is somewhat crippled. No wonder then that those who win freedom are often unable to use it; no wonder that liberty brings its despair.

There are people who think that rebellion is an inevitable accompaniment of progress. I don't see why it should be. If it is possible to destroy, as I think we are doing, the very basis of authority, then change becomes a matter of invention and deliberate experiment. No doubt there is a long road to travel before we attain such a civilization. But it seems to me that we have every right to look forward to it—to a time when childhood will cease to be assaulted by bogeys, when eagerness for life will cease to be a sin. There is no more reason why everyone should go through the rebellions of our time than that everyone should have to start a suffrage movement to secure his vote.

To idealize rebellion is simply to make a virtue out of necessity. It shows more clearly than anything else that the sheer struggle for freedom is an exhausting thing, so exhausting that the people who lead it are often unable to appreciate its uses. But just as the men who founded democracy were more concerned with the evils of the kingly system than they were with the possibilities of self-government, so it is with working men and women, and with all those who are in revolt against the subtle tyrannies of the school and the home and the creed. Only with difficulty does the affirmative vision emerge. Each of us contributes to it what he can in the intervals of his battle with surviving absolutisms. The vision is clearer to-day than it was to the rebels of the nineteenth century. We are more used to freedom than they were. But in comparison with what we need our vision is murky, fragmentary, and distorted. We have dared to look upon life naturally, we have exorcised many bogeys and laid many superstitions, we have felt reality bend to our purposes. We gather assurance from these hints.